A Moonrunner's Tale
From Grit to Gold:
How "The Dukes" Was Born

A "MOONRUNNERS" Tale

From Grit to Gold:
How "The Dukes" Was Born

By
Jon Holland

This book has not been licensed, approved, or sponsored by any entity involved in creating or producing *The Dukes of Hazzard* or *Moonrunners*.

This book is dedicated to

the Rushing Family.

Thanks for sharing your stories.

Contents

Director of Photography Brian Roy plans for the next
scene while gaffer Bert Bertolami looks on.
Picture from private collection.

Foreword

As a kid growing up in Scotland, I was fascinated with the process of making movies, the art of story telling via the big screen. It was what I wanted to do with my life, and I have spent the last forty odd years as a cameraman.

The road from the Highlands of Scotland led me to the back roads of Georgia. I moved from the "Highland Fling" to "clog dancing" on a flat bed truck. I left my native Scotch whisky only to discover moonshine. I recall much of the experience with fondness.

Between high speed chases, wrecking cars, making day look like night, and blowing up things like cotton gins and stills, there's little that I've not been surprised by. How much more fun can a grown man have without getting arrested? And to get paid for it? That is the truly amazing part!

Through the years I've learned that there is a huge difference between watching the making of a film on television and experiencing life on a real movie set. Despite some of the challenges that inevitably arise in filming, I still cherish each moment and embrace it with the same desire I had when I first began my career. Moments like Kiel Martin diving into a bevy of reclining beauties while turning in mid air in order to stay in his light make me appreciate the work that goes into a film.

I learned a great deal about my craft while on the set of *Moonrunners*. I was lucky enough to have artistic freedom and the ability to do what I felt needed to be done to capture the emotion and feel that Gy Waldron's script evoked. Waldron and I worked together closely to make sure that it was the truest form of his vision we brought to the screen.

We were assisted greatly in this venture by the locations chosen for the film. There is little doubt in my mind that we could have better captured the grittiness of Southern moonshining culture anywhere else. From the Hagg farmhouse to the local roads, every little detail lent its own charm to the film.

Though the film wrapped nearly forty years ago, several members of the cast and crew still see each other often around the Atlanta area. We've since had the chance to work on many projects and reminisce about our time together in the fall of 1973.

My thanks to everyone. Thanks especially to Jerry Rushing without whom this story couldn't have been told. Thanks also to Jon Holland for keeping *Moonrunners* alive.

Brian W. Roy
January 2010

Introduction

I go to some hollow
And sit at my still
And if whiskey don't kill me
Then I don't know what will.
　　　--Bob Dylan, "Moonshiner"

A tall tale is defined as a story with elements that are so exaggerated they are unbelievable. For example, some of the most notorious American tall tales are centered around Pecos Bill, a legendary cowboy who was said to have tamed the Wild West. In fact, one such story recounts the time that ol' Pecos Bill proved once and for all that he could ride anything.[1] You see, Pecos Bill was traveling through Kansas when he made up his mind he was going to ride a tornado. So he waited for the "biggest gol-durned tornado you ever saw." When that big ol' tornado got ready to pass him, Pecos Bill reached up and grabbed it, pushing it to the ground and jumping right up on its back. The story goes that the tornado gave Pecos Bill one heckuva ride all the way to California where it just rained itself out to nothing.

Pecos Bill was joined by a cast of colorful characters ranging from John Henry to Paul Bunyan. Many of the men and women in these tales really existed, most sharing their story with the Wild West or the American Frontier, a place of danger and excitement. Additionally, many historians believe some of their 'tales' do actually have their roots in the truth.

These days, we don't hear many stories about men who ride tornados or race steam powered hammers and win. We do hear of other such legends, however. Many of these legends take root in decades much closer to our own. In 1965, Tom Wolfe wrote an article for *Esquire* about one of those legends. In fact, Wolfe went as far as dubbing this man "the last American hero."[2] This 'hero' was not a wild cowboy, and he did not embrace the frontier culture, but he did represent a whole class of people who for hundreds of years had been pushed down and back and all but pushed out. This 'hero' was the legendary Junior Johnson, NASCAR champion and North Carolina bootlegger.

Wolfe's article chronicled Johnson's rise to NASCAR fame. Leaving no detail out, Wolfe covered Johnson's life from the poverty stricken family he was raised in to his landing in a federal penitentiary for making moonshine. Ultimately, Wolfe's article targeted the skills Johnson acquired in the backwoods that enable him to make racing history. Wolfe articulately and excitedly related the story of a legendary North Carolinian that many held close to their own heart. Junior Johnson was a legend to so many Southern boys because he was able to do just what they dreamt of: leave the dirt roads and moonshine behind for asphalt tracks and racing trophies. The dreams of these boys, along with Johnson's reality, fueled stories like *Last American Hero* and *The Dukes of Hazzard*.

These stories reinforced the truth that moonshining was a deep rooted part of Southern culture that could not be ignored. The production and transportation of illegal corn whiskey was both the victor and the villain of many Southern families. To ignore that part of Southern heritage is to discredit the practices that allowed so many to survive during the dark years of Reconstruction and the Great Depression. Through these stories, the image of a Southern hero emerges.

A Moonrunners Tale is one of these stories. It is the story of how one moonrunner managed to become an American tall tale or, if you prefer, a bona fide American hero.

The South and Her Likker

Moonshine

The Oxford English Dictionary describes "moonshine" as "a trifle; nothing." Its colloquial usage as a term to describe "smuggled or illicitly distilled alcoholic liquor" seems to have its origins in England. In 1785, Francis Grose wrote in his *A Classical Dictionary of the Vulgar Tongue*, "the white brandy smuggled on the coasts of Kent and Sussex is called moonshine."[5] Some assume the name is derived from the evening hours that many smugglers chose to practice their profession. Perhaps explanations even took the form as "Oh that box? That's mere moonshine," meaning, "that's nothing. Simply the moon's reflection." Though the true origin of the word may never be known, moonshine has come to refer to any distilled spirit made in an unlicensed still. The process used to produce this alcohol is simple: yeast ferments sugar to produce ethanol, then alcohol is extracted through distillation using a still.

The danger with this backwoods tonic is that it can often have impurities. Because stills are not regulated by law, there is not a defined process for production. Many moonshines pick up impurities from unclean filtering devices, including car radiators. Other toxins, such as methanol (denatured alcohol) are added during the process. Moonshines with high concentrations of methanol are likely to cause blindness and even death.

Ancient History

The distillation of whiskey is nothing new. In fact, the first recorded use of a still was in Persia in the ninth century. Noted alchemist Jabir ibn Hayyan created an alembic still and began the process of distilling wine.[3] He described the resulting ethanol as having little use, but being significant in the advancement of science. Soon after, Persian scientist Al-Razi began using ethanol in medicine. Despite its practical uses, it seemed the enjoyment of this pure alcohol was already catching on. Persian poet Abu Nuwas described the liquid as having "the color of rain-water, but [being] as hot inside the ribs as a burning firebrand."[4]

As trade increased over vast territories, the distillation of alcohol spread quickly throughout continental Europe and Asia, rising in popularity rapidly. Many countries used their indigenous alcoholic beverages to produce this pure substance. Its inclusion in medicine was invaluable throughout the world, and it furthered the field of alchemy (chemistry) significantly. The tools used by scientists, doctors, and pleasure seekers have varied little in the last thousand years. Stills can be exceedingly complex, but most have retained a structure similar to the one used by Hayyan.

The Whiskey Insurrection

The struggle between good ol' boy entrepreneurs and the federal government has been passed down for generations, beginning in the first years of the foundation of the United States of America. Alexander Hamilton, the first Secretary of the Treasury, urged the national government to assume the debt that states incurred during the Revolutionary War. In 1791, following this assumption of debt, Hamilton suggested that a tax be placed on alcohol and carriages to offset some of the nation's debt. The law was to be "more of a social discipline than as a source of revenue."[5] Furthermore, it was thought that if the national government was to impose such a tax it would "advance and secure [Its] power."[6]

The alcohol tax was designed to crush the little guy. Small distillers would pay roughly nine cents per gallon, whereas large distilleries could pay a flat rate of six cents per gallon. There was an obvious bias, and many small producers felt it was no coincidence that President George Washington, owner of a large distillery, happened to support the tax.

The small farmer on the western borders of the United States was stuck. It was impossible in some locations to transport corn or wheat into a town with a market. Because of this lack of infrastructure, farmers were forced to turn to the most profitable means of harvest: the production of liquor. The liquor produced could be sold or used for barter or exchange for other goods and services. The alcohol tax of 1791 was detrimental to the farmers who were essentially forced to produce alcohol as a means of survival.

Over the summer of 1794, tensions truly began to mount between the small farm distillers and the national government. The government tax collectors sent to the western regions of Pennsylvania to collect their alcohol tax were met with hostility and violence. The violence grew to such a peak that bands of small producers were reported to have tarred and feathered a tax collector who was attempting to enforce Hamilton's law.[7]

It was at this time that President Washington ordered federal marshals to serve court orders. After federal marshals were unable to get these militants to appear in court, Washington took matters into his own hands, summoning the militias of Virginia, Pennsylvania, and other bordering states. He organized a group of more than 12,900 men and commanded this army alongside Alexander Hamilton and Harry "Lighthorse" Lee. These men marched first to Bedford, Pennsylvania and then on to the western areas of Pennsylvania that had seen the most protest.

It was October 1794 when Washington arrived to punish the offenders. Key members of the rouge group were never found, though Washington's army managed to arrest twenty men, demonstrating the Federalist authority of the national government for the first time. Eventually, all but one man (he died in prison) were pardoned by President Washington. The event culminated with fines and charges for "assisting and abetting in setting up seditious pole in opposition to the laws of the United States."[8] In January 1796, these fines were served to 26 men of Pennsylvania, and the issue was pushed aside.

Hamilton's law was repealed in 1803 because it was essentially unenforceable outside western Pennsylvania. (The United States capitol was located in Philadelphia, Pennsylvania at this time.) In fact, farmers in areas of Kentucky and Tennessee were encouraged to increase their own productions because they were too far removed from the nation's capital to be caught or taxed. This increased production eventually lead to the creation of Bourbon—a special whiskey made in Kentucky.

The damage caused by the national government's attempt to squelch the outbreak from these small farmers was irreparable for the Federalist party. Many came to see the military reaction to these farmers as being overbearing and unfair. Early Americans were beginning to doubt their newly earned freedom. Was the American government turning into the oppressive monarchy they had just rid themselves of? The skepticism that resulted from the Whiskey Insurrection was met with the formation of the Democratic-Republic party in Washington, which vowed to keep the people's—and in turn the states'—rights in tact.

Prohibition

The next major upset for small distillers came during the Temperance Movement. For centuries, religious groups and governments have attempted to assert control over social or moral behaviors. The consumption of alcohol has, seemingly, always been a target with many groups upholding the idea that excessive consumption leads to physical, psychological, and financial downfall. In addition, many religious groups shun alcohol as a "sinful" beverage that leads people away from the "paths of righteousness."[9] The Temperance Movement in the United States experienced a burst of popularity in the 1800s. In 1826, the American Temperance Society was formed and encouraged citizens to renew their interest in religion and morality.

This organization paved the way for Temperance education from groups like the Women's Christian Temperance Union founded in 1873. In 1880, the WCTU founded a Department of Scientific Temperance Instruction led by Mary Hunt. The mission of this department was to to educate students of the evils of alcohol and narcotics. Hunt believed that voters must see "that alcohol and kindred narcotics are by nature outlaws, before they will outlaw them."[10]

The education of students and voters was wildly successful and by the turn of the twentieth century nearly every state, as well as the District of Columbia, had legislation on the books that mandated temperance education in public schools. This education paved the way for Prohibition. On December 18, 1917, the Eighteenth Amendment to the United States Constitution was proposed; this amendment banned the sale, manufacture, and transportation of alcohol for consumption on a national level.[11] Following ratification on January 16, 1919, the amendment went into effect on January 16, 1920. Prohibition, also known as The Noble Experiment, polarized the country.

Following the ratification of the Eighteenth Amendment, Congress passed the Volstead Act on October 28, 1919, despite President Woodrow Wilson's veto. The Volstead Act, named for Andrew Volstead, Chairman of the House Judiciary Committee, defined "intoxicating liquors" as beverages containing more than 0.5% alcohol and further prohibited the sale of alcohol in the United States.[12] The new legislation, however, did little to curb desires of the people, and the illegal production and distribution of alcohol, known as bootlegging, became rampant. The United States Government did not have the means to enforce the law against every "speakeasy" or "bootlegger" in America.

Prohibition lasted from 1920 to 1933 when dissent from the people became so vocal that President Franklin Delano Roosevelt signed an amendment to the Volstead Act called the Cullen-Harrison Act, saying "I think this would be a good time for a beer."[13] This amendment allowed the production of 3.2 beer (beer with roughly 4% alcohol by volume) and light wines. The Cullen-Harrison Act became a law on April 7, 1933, and in celebration, Anheuser-Busch sent President Roosevelt a case of beer on April 8, 1933. The beer was delivered by a team of the company's famed Clydesdale horses. After President Roosevelt's action, Congress ratified the Twenty-first Amendment a few months later on December 5, 1933; this amendment repealed the Eighteenth Amendment and gave states the right to restrict or ban the sale of alcohol. Prohibition was officially over.

The effects of Prohibition on the nation's economy and society were far more damaging than anyone could have foreseen. Tycoon John D. Rockefeller, a supporter of Prohibition, wrote:

> When Prohibition was introduced, I hoped that it would be widely supported by public opinion and the day would soon come when the evil effects of alcohol would be recognized. I have slowly and reluctantly come to believe that this has not been the result. Instead, drinking has generally increased; the speakeasy has replaced the saloon; a vast army of lawbreakers has appeared; many of our best citizens have openly ignored Prohibition; respect for the law has been greatly lessened; and crime has increased to a level never seen before.[14]

Rockefeller was referring to the rise in organized crime and alcohol trafficking in the United States. Prior to 1920, the Mafia had largely limited its interests to gambling and theft. However, Prohibition opened new doors to the powerful, urban gangs; the selling of illegal alcohol on the black market and the operation of illegal speakeasies was a phenomenal money-maker for these groups. Many groups employed local law enforcement officers and government officials under the table in exchange for immunity from the law. The corruption that resulted from such unethical procedure plagued both local and federal governments for decades.

Liquor and Fast Cars

While organized crime was rampant in the North, a different type of bootlegging was more common in the South. In urban areas, organized groups of criminals would transport "bathtub gin" and other strong homemade alcohols into the city via speakeasies. In rural areas, including vast regions of the South, illegal alcohol, or "moonshine," was often transported by the producer. Rather than selling the illegal product to a syndicate for distribution, small producers would either deliver their own product or hire a local bootlegger to deliver for them.

These delivery men were more doggedly pursued by the federal government than producers were because of the profit that bootleggers often made on their runs. It was during the late 1920s, before the repeal of Prohibition, that many bootleggers began creating high performance stock cars to assist with their deliveries. Often the car's engine and suspension would be modified to provide a stiffer, faster ride. The logic behind these modifications was that a better car would easily be able to outrun a federal agent during pursuit.

Even after Prohibition was overturned, the practice of modifying stock cars to create faster, better vehicles remained commonplace. It was from these shady beginnings that the National Association of Stock Car Auto Racing emerged. What was begun as a method of outrunning the law became one of the South's most revered past times. From the serpentine roads of the Appalachian mountains to the sandy beaches of Daytona, Florida, stock cars were being pushed to their limits. As the stakes rose for drivers, the popularity of racing grew among spectators. In February of 1948, William France, Sr., recognizing the desires of a large fan base, created NASCAR in order to formally organize the sport for both drivers and spectators.[15]

After its formation in Daytona Beach, NASCAR exploded as an international phenomenon, drawing the world's greatest drivers all of whom wanted to test their skills on the short track. Men like Junior Johnson, Richard Petty, and Cale Yarborough became legends on the circuit. For the majority of these drivers, their tenure began on the short dirt tracks in their local area. Racing moved from being a Friday and Saturday night staple to a Sunday afternoon ritual.

Liquor and fast cars are exactly what gave Jerry Rushing his start in the world. Growing up in a moonshining family, there were not many other options for a young boy in the country. Naturally, Rushing followed in his father's footsteps and took great pains to become the best. He moved rapidly from the woods and back roads of Union County, to the dirt tracks of North and South Carolina, and finally came to a stop in Hollywood. Life was never easy, but as Rushing says, "it sure was fun."

One of Rushing's race cars. The fender is inscribed:
"Don't cry, baby. I'm not your boyfriend."
Picture from private collection.

Johnny and Jerry Rushing circa 1980. The pair were the model for cousins Bobby Lee and Grady Hagg and Bo and Luke Duke. Of course, the Rushing boys raised a little more hell than either of their fictitious counterparts. Below, Rushing is sampling his wares. Though the boxes say "Coke," there's no doubt about what's really inside. Like Coke, Rushing Moonshine was "the real thing."

Pictures from private collection.

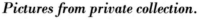

The Original Duke Boy

Born to a poor family in southern North Carolina, Jerry Elijah Rushing would grow up to become a legend on the small screen. His father, Espie, his uncle, John, and his grandfather, Atlas, were famous in Union County for making whiskey. For a young boy growing up in a small, rural town, taking an interest in what the men in your family did was only natural. Around the age of eleven, Jerry began to express his interest in the family business. His father was opposed to Jerry's involvement not only on the grounds of his age, but also because he saw a 'wildness' in his oldest son. Jerry remembers his father telling him that "[he] was too crazy to learn how to make liquor." The senior Rushing believed that Jerry would likely get "too big" and end up getting caught like so many other large moonshine producers.

The young Jerry was not dissuaded by his father's opposition. He was persistent in his efforts to convince his father that he could do it, and, eventually, it was that persistence that paid off. Jerry's first taste of the family business was actually at his father's request: Espie Rushing sent his twelve year old son to get a bottle of shine from John "Worley" Rushing, Jerry's uncle. It was that day when Jerry realized what he wanted to do with his life.

After boasting to his friends for a few years that he would become a moonshine hauler, Jerry finally had a chance to prove himself. As he drove to his Uncle Worley's, Jerry imagined he was outrunning a revenue agent. At the age of twelve, he was already a pretty good driver and admittedly liked the thrill and rush of a car chase. As he drove to his uncle's at breakneck speeds, he drew attention to his old truck, but ended up making the trip there without any problems. He picked up the jar of shine and took care to wrap the glass with burlap so it would not rattle or break under his seat. The young teen then headed back to his own home, traveling the same roads he used on his way there. In the few miles between his uncle's house and his own, Jerry was spotted by local law enforcement, and a pursuit began. Jerry finally had the chance to make his boyhood fantasy a reality.

Having driven the curvy dirt roads between the two farms for many years and having watched his father get into the same jams, Jerry figured he knew what to do. He pushed that old truck to its limits, watching all the while as the speedometer needle crept higher and higher. Within a few minutes, Jerry managed to evade the law. He headed home and delivered his "load" with the knowledge that it would be the first of many.

Soon, Jerry became an apprentice to his uncle. It was no secret in Union County that Worley Rushing made some of the best moonshine in North Carolina. Before long, Jerry began to haul shine for his uncle. After months of hauling and lots of questions, Jerry began to learn the art of whiskey production from Worley as well. Jerry was fearless and determined. He had three distinct goals by fourteen: he wanted to be the fastest, the biggest, and the best. And he was well on his way.

Jerry was never a drinker; he was a maker. He learned to have a sense of pride in his product and a sense of respect for what the product could do to a man. He learned these lessons at his uncle's side. Jerry fondly remembers Worley taking care of his stills "the way a woman would care for her frying pans." He would polish the copper frequently with steel wool. He would use the choicest and purest corn or fruit to create his mash. Worley also made sure to take great care in using a pure filtration system. He bottled only in glass, and he often aged his whiskey to create the best possible product.

Jerry watched and learned. He paid attention to time honored practices, and he made sure he could replicate those practices. By sixteen, Jerry was running his own whiskey made in his own stills. It was 1953, and Jerry Elijah Rushing was officially a third generation moonshiner. He did not do all the work himself though; like many other moonshiners, Jerry had a fleet of "souped up" cars to help him along the way.

The first car that Jerry remembers using regularly to haul whiskey was a 1942 Chevrolet coupe. Often moonshiners, like Jerry, would beef up the suspension and fine tune the motor on their hauling cars to give them better performance. The last thing any bootlegger wanted was a slow ride. Revenuers were prone to comment that there was no real competition between their cars and the cars of bootleggers; bootleggers always had more money to invest in their vehicles, while revenuers relied on government issued cars. Because the bootleggers ran their cars constantly at such high levels of performance, the cars never lasted that long. Also, haulers would switch cars out frequently to keep federal agents from being able to keep tabs on their activity.

Though unsure of the exact number, Jerry estimates he used between fifteen and twenty cars during his career as a bootlegger. While each of the cars had its charms, there were two vehicles that hold a special place in his heart: a 1955 Ford truck and a 1958 Chrysler 300D.

Jerry's 1955 Ford truck was a workhorse. It could haul supplies better than any of his other vehicles. The doors of the cab were painted to advertise "Jerry's Archery Lanes," the legal business Jerry conducted by day. When not being used to haul archery supplies, furs, or traps, Jerry used the truck to haul sugar to and from still sites. With careful packing, 76 bags of sugar could be loaded in the bed of the old truck.

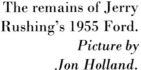

The remains of Jerry Rushing's 1955 Ford.
Picture by Jon Holland.

His truck had more practical uses, but the 1958 Chrysler 300D was Jerry's breadwinner, serving as his primary bootlegging car. A Southerner to his core, Jerry named the white vehicle "Traveler" after Confederate General Robert E. Lee's horse. Traveler was equipped with a Chrysler FirePower engine: a 392 cubic inch raised deck block with a hemispherical combustion head. Ranging from 325 to 345 horsepower in its stock form and utilizing two four-barrel carburetors, Jerry had one of the highest performing cars on the road in the early 1960s.

Jerry was not the only bootlegger to recognize the power the 300D held; it was a popular choice for many moonshiners. There was a difference between Jerry Rushing and the other moonshiners however: driving ability. Traveler belonged to another whisky producer prior to Jerry. ATF agents confiscated the hot car on a raid, and like most confiscated property, it was auctioned off to the public. Jerry acquired Traveler at the auction for $155.00; he remembers that no one else dared to bid against him.

Traveler, Jerry Rushing's favorite moon hauler.
Picture by Jon Holland.

Pure power.
Picture by Jon Holland.

"I drove Traveler about 125,00 miles and only spent a dollar and a quarter on him," Jerry recalls. "I could haul 300 gallons in Traveler, and he would grip and hold right on the road like a dream," he smiles, "it was one of the best cars I ever owned." After he acquired the car, Jerry had Traveler rigged with several options to keep him well ahead of revenue agents and local law enforcement officers. One of the more clever tricks Jerry had up his sleeve involved the brake lights: the lights were rewired to be controlled by a button; one push and the lights would be disabled. This allowed Jerry to hit the brakes in his car, but give no indication to following cars that he was doing so. Jerry remembers: "One time I was being chased around a dirt road with some very sharp turns. Since the cops never saw my brake lights they never knew when to apply their brakes. When I would slow down on turns, they would just run right over the cliff." Jerry often compared the headlights of pursing cars to "flashlights bouncing through the woods."

In addition to his rigged brake lights, Jerry had a "slick" trick that he liked to use when cars got a little too close. The trunk of Traveler was customized to hold an oil dump tank. This would be filled with motor oil, which when applied to the road would cause the pursuing vehicle to lose control and slide off the road. The oil was released through a small tube mounted near the exhaust pipe and was controlled by a toggle switch on the dashboard.

Behind the wheel of Rushing's 1958 Chrysler 300 D.

Picture by Jon Holland.

Traveler was able to fit over 300 carefully packed gallons of moonshine.

Picture by Jon Holland.

"I've driven through corn fields, barbed wire fences, and barns. I've been shot at and listened to bullets bounce around inside the car. I hit countless things and just kept on going," Jerry laughs. While Jerry remembers getting into all sorts of scrapes in Traveler with fondness, his separation from the car still causes him pain. A car to a moonshiner is a partner, and a good car, like Traveler, becomes even greater, almost an extension of the man himself. Late one night, Jerry ran and ran, but was not able to out run. Jerry was running a new route, and the oil pump in Traveler stopped working. He abandoned the car so that he could escape to safety.

Normally, bootleggers would return for their car if it was ever left along the way; Jerry, however, was notorious, and federal agents watched Traveler like a hawk, waiting for his return. Rather than risk his own capture, Jerry let the car go, and agents eventually got tired of watching the car they'd spent so long pursuing sit still. Traveler was hauled to an impound yard to waste away. Many years later, Bob Dupin, the founder of the Chrysler 300 Club rescued Traveler and sold him to Richard Dangler, a New York lawyer. Dangler (with a team of body men and mechanics) restored the car to its original state. Now, Traveler is owned by Larry Wolfel of Connecticut. While he never got his car back, Jerry knows that "Traveler never let [him] down."

Soon after Jerry abandoned Traveler, his father's worst fear was realized: Jerry was busted by the feds. Jerry's bottle producer was busted on the way to a still site. To clear himself, he informed the feds of the still and where it was located. On September 1, 1962, federal agents raided a still in Union County on the property of L. Williams. The still was hidden inside a barn, which had been covered with tarpaper to mask the light inside. Pine oil disinfectant was sprinkled around the building to cover the smell of liquor. The 1,000 gallon still was found and destroyed along with the 392 gallons of liquor in it.

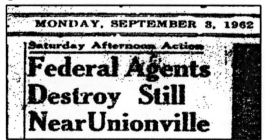

The headline of *The Monroe Enquirer* announced the capture of the still by federal agents on Monday, September 3,

Jerry's partner, Williams, was captured on the property and arrested for the production of moonshine. During the bust, this gentleman was cuffed on site and held while the alcohol was destroyed. Jerry remembers hearing later that as agents busted each jug of liquor, his partner would call out $5.00, which was the going price for a gallon in those days. This particular still was able to produce about 400 gallons a day, garnering around $14,000 a week.

While Jerry was not directly connected with the still, his associate turned Jerry's name in to authorities in an attempt to have his sentence reduced. Jerry was not made to serve time in prison, however, he was placed on probation for five years. The bust was significant, as the still was the largest one of its kind ever to be captured. After the allegations and proceedings concluded in 1965, Jerry scaled back his involvement in the liquor business significantly, turning his attentions back to archery and taxidermy.

One of the first changes Jerry made to his business was the removal of any non-family members. This forced Jerry to cut production back from the thousands of gallons he had been producing each week. At one point, Jerry was operating eleven stills, using one for a week or two, then switching to another, and so on. He focused on operations closer to his home base and worked closely with his brother Johnny. By the early 1970s, Jerry had practically ceased producing liquor and concentrated on transporting it. He claims that's where the true money was made. Bootleggers would often pay a producer $5.00 a gallon, only to turn around and sell it for $10.00 or $12.00 a gallon. The overage was pure profit.

Jerry became known as the "Big Hat Man" because of the large black Stetson he always wore. His customers knew his face, his hat, and his car, but they would never know his name. Jerry preferred the anonymity; a moonshiner could never be too careful.

Picture from private collection.

In addition to his liquor deliveries, Jerry set up a small Western town to house his fur and taxidermy businesses. He also operated an archery range, selling mostly Bear Archery products. Jerry and his wife, Dean, were both involved in archery competitions. The pair was nationally acclaimed and even offered sponsorships from Bear. Their notoriety gained a certain amount of attention, and the business thrived. Jerry soon added a small bar to the town, entertaining friends and customers with poker games, pool tables, and moonshine by the shot. The bar was dubbed the "Boarsnest" and became the official home of the Sherwood Bow Club.

The small cabin here was the "jail" of Sherwood.

The cinder block building seen here housed the Sherwood Bow Club and "Boarsnest" bar.

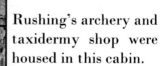

Rushing's archery and taxidermy shop were housed in this cabin.

Pictures by Jon Holland.

An avid fan of Jesse James and other outlaws of the Wild Wild West, Jerry wanted to create a sense of authenticity on his little piece of property. He built a jail to house those who got a little too rowdy during evening festivities. Occasionally, he and his friends would stage shoot outs on the path outside of the buildings in the middle of "town." Truly a kid at heart, Jerry would also play "Cowboys and Indians," pitching teepees in the field across from the Boarsnest.

Jerry's own version of Sherwood Forest (think Robin Hood) would not have been complete without a musical venue. He constructed a small stage in the middle of the complex for him and his friends. Jerry would arrange fiddler's conventions and contract local music groups. One of the first performers on Jerry's stage was Randy Traywick, now known as Randy Travis. Travis's father and Jerry rode horses together. Jerry even had a still on Travis's grandfather's property at one point.

One of the first stages Randy Travis ever used.
Picture by Jon Holland.

All of these buildings have since fallen into disrepair, but at one point, this small area was the home to Jerry and all of his moonshiner friends. Strangers were not welcome in the area, as has been the case in the Appalachian region for many years. Jerry recalls, with particular fondness, an afternoon visit from the president of the local bank: "We were all sitting in the bow shop when a car no one recognized pulled up, and two men in suits climbed out. Every old boy in that room slowly eased their hand on their gun. All you could hear was the sound of hammers pulling back. Those two men had the mess scared out of them. I tried to explain that the only people to wear suits around there were federal agents, but it didn't matter. The bank president told me it was the last time he'd ever bring me a box of candy or pay a visit!"

Despite changes in profession (at least outwardly), one thing remained constant in Jerry's life: a love of music. Initially, Jerry's passion for music arose out of necessity; he would write songs to pass the time while delivering liquor. "When the moon was full and shining on those liquor jars as they rattled in the back, man, that's when I could really write a song," comments Jerry. He would drive and sing, making late nights flow into early mornings. His talent was obvious; Jerry penned many tunes that were considered by multiple Country and Western artists for production. There was one song in particular, however, that had a special significance for Jerry. He felt that it was a story that needed to be told and a story that many would be able to identify with. It was called "Mama Had to Pay."

"Mama Had to Pay"
Jerry E. Rushing

I heard my mama beg the judge,
"Please don't take my little boy away.
Give him just one more chance.
Let me take him home today.
He's not a bad boy.
He's just a little wild.
Please I beg of you, don't take my only child."

Well Mama was getting old,

And it was hard to understand.
That her little boy had grown into a full grown man.
Making moonshine whiskey was the only trade he had.
Just a reckless country boy,
Walking in the footsteps of his dad.
Well my throat tightened as I thought back today.
But the worst part of all: my Mama had to pay.

"Judge, please don't take my boy away.
Give him just one more chance.
Let me take him home today.
He's not a bad boy.
He's just a little wild.
Please I beg of you.
Don't take my only child."

Well my dad taught me the trade,
And he must have taught me well,
Between the two of us,
We made Mama's life a living hell.
Then one day my dad was called away.
He died from drink, but Mama had to pay.
"He's not a bad boy.
He's just a little wild,
Please I beg of you.
Don't take my only child."

I can remember my daddy,
Making whiskey, till way late at night.
And mom would sit there by the window,
Watching for his old lantern light.
Then dad died, and I took up the trade.
Not really knowing, I was putting Mama in her grave.
Then it didn't seem all that bad.
I was just keeping up an old family tradition,
Walking in the footsteps of my dear old dad.
Then one day the law came and took me away.
I was all she had left in the world.
So once again, Mama had to pay.

I guess it was just too much for Mama,
Being left all alone,
Then one dark night,
The Lord came and called Mama home.
I stood there, tears falling down,
As I watched them lower dear old Mama
In the cold, cold ground.
And those last words,
I can still hear today,
"Please don't take my little boy away."

Hoping for a break out of Union County, Jerry took the song to a local lawyer with many connections in the music industry. Jerry didn't get the response he expected, but he did step through a door that catapulted him from local moonshiner and bootlegger to internationally known legend.

Moonrunners: From Grit to Gold

Robert B. Clark, a lawyer based in Monroe, North Carolina, had no idea what was in store for him the day Jerry Rushing walked into his office. Rushing had a song he wanted published, and while Clark had connections in the music industry, he did not feel it was the right place for Jerry Rushing. Clark had a friend working as a screenwriter in Atlanta. His current script was about a family of moonshiners, but it lacked grit and color. After reading the lyrics of "Mama Had to Pay," Clark sized up the tall roughneck standing in front of him and knew he had just hit pay dirt. Turning down Rushing's song, Clark asked him to go home and write some stories about moonshining instead. Rushing was floored: "Man, I can't write all that stuff down. It's just the way I live." The men talked it through, and it was decided that Rushing would tell his stories and record them on tape.

For several evenings, Rushing talked to a machine about life in Union County and the liquor business. He reminisced about the chase, getting busted, and living life on the edge. He shared stories about his brother and some of their more dangerous adventures. He recalled his favorite cars and his desire to be the fastest bootlegger on the road. Rushing told the recorder of his love for his family and his reason for choosing this life for himself. When he was done, he collected the tapes and took them back to Clark's office. It was far better than anyone could have imagined; Clark was stunned. "There's enough here for a ten year series!" he exclaimed. Not one for wasting time, Clark contacted the screenwriter and shipped the tapes to him for review. It did not take long for the screenwriter, Gy Waldron, to contact Rushing and request permission to see firsthand how a moonshiner lived and worked.

Rushing agreed to the visit, and Waldron stayed with Clark in Monroe for a week, driving out to Jerry's each day. It was an education in the South for Waldron. Rushing walked him through the process of making liquor step-by-step. Waldron learned how sugar was procured and delivered to still sites. He then witnessed how mash was produced and aged. On another day, Rushing took him to various stills he owned and operated in the area, showing him how the aged mash was turned into liquor. Waldron was also introduced to the art of bootlegging, learning about many of Rushing's tricks to lose pursuers. At the end of his visit, Waldron approached the idea of using elements from Rushing's life in his script. Rushing agreed.

Waldron worked quickly to retool the dry script he'd originally written, turning out what he called *Moonrunners.* Waldron used much of what he'd seen while with Rushing and many of the stories that Rushing had recorded prior to his visit. The script was molded into the story of a moonshining family out to preserve their traditions and their integrity. It was everything that Waldron's original script was not, thanks to Rushing's influence.

By the middle of 1973, Clark, Waldron, and Rushing had formed a partnership and a gentleman's agreement regarding the script. Waldron would be credited as writer and director, Clark would be titled executive producer, and Rushing would serve as technical advisor. In addition, the men agreed that profits, royalties, and rights would be split three ways equally at 33 percent. This agreement lasted through filming and into post-production until Clark and Waldron involved United Artists in 1974. United Artists was hired to release the film and rights were transferred from Moonrunners Limited Partnership (the trio's name) to United Artists. A clause was worked into the deal allowing Moonrunners Ltd Partnership to maintain the creative rights and licensing for potential future developments.

All seemed to be moving forward accordingly for *Moonrunners.* Major characters were cast in Los Angeles, while secondary roles were filled in Atlanta using a great number of local actors. Locations scouts scoured the Georgia countryside, ultimately finding their perfect Shiloh County in Haralson. Waldron hired an expert crew from the Atlanta area and enlisted veteran Brian W. Roy as director of photography for the picture. The cast and crew set up camp at a Holiday Inn in nearby Griffin, and on Monday, September 17, 1973, filming began.

The cast and crew worked on location in Haralson and Williamson for six straight weeks, having only Mondays and the occasional Sunday off. The motto of the group was "work hard, play hard," and lifetime bonds were formed. Rushing remained on set throughout the duration of filming to advise Waldron. In addition, Rushing was cast to perform many of the driving stunts in the film. Seeing Hollywood for the first time, Rushing was entranced by the experience. He involved many people from his hometown in the film, including his best friend Jim Hogan of Norfolk, Virginia, and a mechanic from Monroe, Frank Harris. Hogan primarily worked with the second unit stunt crew while Harris stayed busy as the on-site mechanic and body man.

One man in particular was an asset to the crew as they filmed in Haralson. He was a local cotton farmer and landowner and found the idea of a film crew in his hometown exhilarating. William Estes, known to friends and family as "Bill," offered his land and assistance to the crew just as soon as they arrived in Haralson. His hospitality and friendly demeanor were the epitome of Southern gentility, and he was highly respected by everyone. "Mr. Estes enjoyed every moment the cast and crew were in town," recalls Frank Wilkinson, Estes's son-in-law. From the Hagg farmhouse to Jake Rainey's barbeque, Estes was involved. Even Jake's Cadillac was Estes's daily driver!

On set with the crew of *Moonrunners.*
Picture from private collection.

Despite his willingness to cooperate with the film crew, Wilkinson still remembers that the crew's presence could be inconvenient. *Moonrunners* was filmed in September and October, harvest season for much of the South. The owners and operators of a cotton gin, both Estes and Wilkinson were usually overrun in the fall with both the harvesting and ginning process. "Mid-October is the busiest time for a cotton farmer," Wilkinson explains, "because you are harvesting your crop and trying to process it as quickly as possible. It seemed we had to constantly stop that October because the crew would need to shoot in a certain place or at a certain time."

The crew not only interrupted Wilkinson's ginning schedule, but also destroyed some of his crop. Waldron felt that using a corn field for a chase scene would add an air of excitement and authenticity, as Rushing had often recounted running from the law at all costs. Needing an open field with corn and finding few in cotton country, the crew decided to use a field they found on Wilkinson's property without asking for permission. That afternoon when Wilkinson returned home, he discovered the remnants of the chase and surveyed his damaged crop. "I was most definitely upset, especially considering that the crew had not asked my permission," Wilkinson recalls. The matter was resolved quickly, however, and Wilkinson was paid for his inconvenience and the damage.

The crew took care to make sure no other property was intentionally damaged during the rest of the shoot. The cotton gin that was blown up in near by Williamson was done so with the permission of the owner, W.H. Adamson, who wanted to destroy the building anyway. The bar that Bobby Lee backs into was actually part of a building that was being demolished for reconstruction. The two stills blown up in the film were created for the sole purpose of being destroyed. The crew became extremely cautious, and that cautiousness served them well. The only property they really had left to worry about was the fleet of cars used in filming.

Approximately ten cars were used on the set of *Moonrunners*, and director Gy Waldron was very aware of the risks the stunt crew was taking. Rather than letting a car that had been destroyed continue in the film, it was retired and replaced. Many of the vehicles had double lives; a 1971 Chevy would be a moonrunner one day and a police car the next. Even the star cars had double lives and were gradually wiped out on set. Frank Harris had his hands full working day and night to paint and repair vehicles for filming. Much of the work was done on location as Harris was a native to Monroe, North Carolina and had no shop in the area.

Waldron was mostly able to maintain continuity in the film with the cars' deterioration. The only major inconsistency comes at the film's end when Beth's car is seen at the ruins of Jake's cotton gin wearing its original red paint (the car had been painted yellow earlier in the film). As with real life, the cars wore the wounds they obtained in filming rather than having them magically erased. Toward the end of the film when Zeebo comes to visit Bobby Lee and Grady, this authenticity is clearly seen; Zeebo's car has suffered major damage, and the door is unable to close without help from Zeebo. Little details like this one significantly enhance the gritty reality of the film.

Reality wasn't just seen in the film; Clark and Waldron soon faced the enormous cost of production despite *Moonrunners'* low budget status. Without the financial backing of a studio, Waldron and Clark were responsible for securing their own funding either through personal investment or the wooing of benefactors. With Waldron on set daily, the responsibility of funding was left to Clark, as is typically the case with producers. Unfortunately, Clark was unable to find investors and resorted to other methods for creating cash flow.

While producing *Moonrunners*, Clark still maintained his practice in Monroe. He primarily focused on estate planning and civil proceedings, rarely entering a courtroom for criminal cases. During this time, Clark was managing the estate of a wealthy widow in the area. Feeling mounting pressure because of his inability to line up investors, Clark forged several checks from his client's account to Moonrunners Ltd. Partnership. He assumed he would be able to fund the film and quickly turn the money back over to her account once the flick was released. As he was the account's manager, he figured the missing cash would go largely unnoticed.

A total of three checks were forged by Clark.[15] The first, written on October 27, 1973, was for $20,000.00. On November 12, 1973, another check was penned for $30,000.00. The last check was written just two weeks later on November 26 for $3,000.00. It was nearly six months before the forgery surfaced. The irony was the client whose money Clark "borrowed" had been represented by Clark in a previous case of forgery. Clark fought her initial case in court and won a sizeable settlement. Charges were pressed on June 17, 1974; Clark was released on $5,000.00 bond, and a trial was scheduled for December. By this point, Clark had already left Union County and moved to Atlanta, taking his practice with him.

Clark Gets Suspended Sentence For Forgery

By DOLORES LAVELLE
Staff Writer

A former local attorney pled guilty to two counts of forgery five on the condition that he forfeit his license to practice law in North Carolina and make restitution within eight months to the estate of John Martin the

The attorney had successfully represented Mrs. Martin in a suit against a local contractor, William Carter, in the first such suit in this state wherein the

Monroe Enquirer staff reporter Delores Lavelle covered the trial in the paper's Thursday, December 19 edition.
Image courtesy of The Monroe Enquirer.

The Clark forgery scandal broke just as United Artists picked up the option to release the film. What was unfortunate for Clark became even more unfortunate for his partners in Moonrunners Ltd. who were about to find themselves with significantly lower paychecks. United Artists used house lawyer Shelton Friedman to draw up royalty and rights contracts for Waldron and Clark. Rushing, who was used to a man's word being worth something, was practically cut out of the deal entirely. His initial 33 percent was reduced to a mere eight percent. A small price for Waldron and Clark to pay to a man whose life fueled their story. Rushing, who was not used to Hollywood wheeling and dealing, accepted their offer as it stood and moved on with his life.

The film was released by United Artists on November 8, 1974 and premiered at George Ellis's (Jake Rainey) Film Forum at Ansley Mall in Atlanta. Jim Mitchum (Grady), Pete Munro (Zeebo), Rushing, and Ellis all appeared at the film's opening. Waylon Jennings, the highest grossing actor in *Moonrunners*, also attended the opening in Atlanta. Despite celebrity endorsement (Jenning's inclusion in the film and advertising was phenomenal), the film was received with mixed reviews. Many critics praised the skill of screen legend Arthur Hunnicutt while bashing the lackluster writing and direction of novice Gy Waldron.

After its release in the Atlanta area, United Artists invested in heavy television and print marketing, opening the film to the rest of the United States on May 14, 1975. The new print campaign placed a heavy focus on actor James Mitchum, son of the screen legend Robert Mitchum. The family connection also lent itself to a

James Mitchum and Jerry Rushing toured in 1974 and 1975 to promote *Moonrunners* as it debuted in various locales. Mitchum operated a horse and cattle ranch and the time and made fast friends with Rushing. The pair planned to work together again on *King of the Mountain* with producer Bob Clark, but the project fell apart after filming began.

Picture from private collection.

direct comparison with the 1958 hit *Thunder Road,* hailed by critic Leonard Maltin as "the definitive moonshine picture."[16] United Artists capitalized on the connection by adding the following tag line to the promotional materials: "*Thunder Road* was only a practice run. This is the real thing!'"

Critics, however did not take the bait, and slammed the film, citing that the colorful story was lost in the watered down dialogue. Notorious entertainment publication *Variety* praised Jennings' performance, but cited that "aside from some hairy cross-country auto chases, the picture has little to recommend it."[17] *Los Angeles Times* critic Kevin Thomas proclaimed the film "discursive," but added that it was evident "Waldron really does care about his people and expresses feelings with a certain ease and even, at times, with eloquence."[18] Praise aside, audiences confirmed what critics asserted; the film did not draw the large market that was hoped for. Despite unfavorable reviews and returns in the United States, *Moonrunners* opened in January 1976 in the Philippines and Sweden and fared better than expected. The rich story about a moonshine family was a novelty in these areas, and audiences responded well to the major players.

Waldron was frustrated at the mere $8 million that *Moorunners* grossed at the box office. Very little of that money floated his way as United Artists had constructed a locked contract, blocking much of the profit from Waldron and Clark. After his perceived failure, Waldron returned to the small screen, writing for a smattering of shows including *One Day at a Time*. It was on the set of *One Day at a Time* that Waldron received his break into Hollywood. His writing attracted the attention of producer Norman Lear. Lear was a heavyweight in Hollywood, having produced shows such as *All in the Family* and *Sandford and Son*. Waldron was quickly hired by Lear as a writer for several of Lear's television sitcoms. Through this venue, Phil Mandelker, a producer at Warner Brothers Television, found Waldron and offered him the chance to write a pilot. Waldron handed Mandelker a copy of *Moonrunners*, unintentionally selling the producer on a show with a comic twist. It was 1978, and *The Dukes of Hazzard* was born.

The major changes Waldron put in place for *The Dukes of Hazzard* included a new location and a new cast of characters. Waldron did not, however, have to look far for inspiration. He still relied heavily on Rushing's stories. Despite the obvious connection, Rushing was once again shouldered out of royalties by Waldron and Clark. Initially, this denial was in exchange for Rushing's fulfillment of the role of Cooter Davenport, the jack-leg mechanic of Hazzard County. Waldron's offer of the role to Rushing was out of context. "Warner Brothers was the acting producer, not United Artists and not Gy Waldron. They told me that they would 'pick who [they] wanted' for the roles," Rushing remarked. Rushing later found out that Ben Jones had already been cast for the role of Cooter by an Atlanta casting company.

Rushing on the set of *The Dukes of Hazzard* with football star Claude Humphrey.

Picture from private collection.

After much negotiation, Rushing was offered the part of Ace Parker in the episode "Repo Men." Waldron assured him the role would be recurring. Based on the advice of his lawyers, Rushing accepted the role and planned to move forward with his law suit after filming concluded.

Rushing traveled to the Atlanta area in December 1978 to film "Repo Men." He was treated like royalty on the set, being offered the same star treatment as rising stars Catherine Bach and John Schneider. "People kept introducing me as 'the man of the hour,' referring to the fact they were here because of my life. John [Schneider] and Tom [Wopat] told me they would make sure I got credit," recalls Rushing. Sadly, that credit never materialized. Rushing finished shooting the episode, and Ace Parker never made a reappearance on the series.

After a lengthy legal battle with Clark and Waldron and Warner Brothers Television, Rushing eventually proved his point and was awarded a cut of the profits. He earned a small check from each episode of *The Dukes of Hazzard* that never truly justified his contribution. In 2005, Rushing found himself back in court battling Warner Brothers on *The Dukes of Hazzard* feature film. The case was paramount in the entertainment industry and has been used as a precedent for copyright violation since.[19]

Clark and Waldron (the primary plaintiffs) asserted that Warner Brothers never purchased the option of releasing a full length feature from United Artists or Moonrunners Ltd. Partnership. Because of Warner Brothers's negligence, the plaintiffs demanded the film be blocked until they were paid for their creative property. Warner Brothers ultimately settled the case because of the loss in revenue they would suffer were the film not released as advertised. While exact details of the settlement are confidential, several sources estimated the deal to come in around $17.5 million.[20] This amount was reportedly larger than the combined salaries of the three leads in the film. The settlement was a significant payday for Waldron and Clark, while Rushing, once again, received an extremely small percentage.

For someone who lived larger than life, the exclusion Jerry Rushing endured from his "partners" was belittling and demeaning. It can be argued that *Moonrunners* was never the creative property of Rushing, but his influence on the film (and subsequently on *The*

Dukes of Hazzard) is undeniable. Rushing's identity fueled the very essence of the two productions from start to finish.

It should be said that men like Rushing are the backbone of the South. He embodies the rugged, hard working nature of man, remaining fiercely devoted to his family and exuding Southern charm and hospitality. In essence, Jerry Rushing is just one of those good old boys never meaning no harm...

A Comparison:
Jerry Rushing vs. *Moonrunners* vs. *The Dukes of Hazzard*

Jerry Rushing	*Moonrunners*	The Dukes of Hazzard
Jerry and Johnny Rushing (brothers)	Bobby Lee and Grady Hagg (cousins)	Bo and Luke Duke (cousins)
Car: Traveler	Car: Traveler	Car: General Lee
Delaine Rushing (cousin)		Daisy Duke (cousin)
Delaine's CB name was Dixie Darling		Daisy's Jeep was named Dixie
Uncle Worley Moonshiner	Uncle Jesse Moonshiner	Uncle Jesse Moonshiner
Best friend Hogan	Friend Cooter	Best friend Cooter
Jerry and Johnny were on probation. Forced to use bows.	Bobby Lee and Grady were on probation. Forced to use bows.	Bo and Luke were on probation. Forced to use bows.
Jerry used YEE-HAW frequently while telling his life story.		The Dukes said YEE-HAW.

Jerry Rushing	*Moonrunners*	*The Dukes of Hazzard*
Kate was Jerry's mule.	Beauregard was Jesse's mule.	Maudine was the Duke's mule.
	Balladeer Waylon Jennings	Balladeer Waylon Jennings
Jerry raced local dirt tracks on the weekend.	Grady raced local dirt tracks.	Bo and Luke raced everywhere and eventually made it to NASCAR.
Local Boss: Juke Brooks	Local Boss: Jake Rainey	Local Boss: Jefferson Davis Hogg

Jerry Rushing with his cousin Delaine. In *The Dukes of Hazzard*, Delaine was the inspiration for Daisy Duke.
Picture from Lawrence Wolfel.

Moonrunners:
A Look Behind the Scenes

"The moon was an accident."

The film begins with poignant narration from Waylon Jennings and a black screen with the simple image of a moon in the top corner. As the narration ends and music begins, the "moon" becomes the headlights of a car moving across the screen.

Director of Photography Brian W. Roy fondly remembers the creation of this opening:

"We were filming the opening sequence outside the Boar's Nest at night. I looked through my camera at the head lights coming down the road, and they were out of focus—the two lights appeared to be one. As they moved closer, I slowly started to focus the camera, and what once looked like a glowing moon, now took on the appearance of the car headlights they were. The script was not supposed to open this way, but what was a complete accident ended up becoming the perfect opening for the film."

"I'm not really a stunt driver."

As the Pickens County deputy and sheriff pull into the parking lot of the Boar's Nest, the police car slides in the gravel, heightening the anxiety of the scene.

John Clower, who played deputy L.D., explains how he lost control of the car as he made the turn:

"To pull into the parking lot of the Boar's Nest, you had to make a right off of the main road. I was going a little too fast when I made that right turn, and just as soon as the tires hit the gravel, the car started to slide left towards the camera. I started to freak out because I wasn't really sure how it was going to end up, and I didn't really know how to stop it. Instinct kicked in, and I hit the brakes and straightened the wheel. The car righted itself and pulled into the parking lot. It made for a really great shot, and the directors seemed to love seeing the police car slide up beside the car we were chasing."

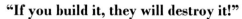

"If you build it, they will destroy it!"

     A small building was being town down in the area section by section. Knowing the limited budget the crew had to work with, art director Pat Mann was able to persuade the demolition crew to give him the section of the building seen above for filming. He needed to create a biker bar that could be destroyed by a car. Mann moved the section of building onto an open space just off of a roadway, using the rails you can just see under the building.

     This made the perfect prop to destroy. The "dumpy" appearance added to the overall gritty mood of the Hell's Angels biker bar, and with a few small details (including some Pabst Blue Ribbon advertisements and booths), Mann managed to create an ideal stage.

     Though Brian Roy remembers the challenges of filming in such a dimly lit space, he also remarks that it added a certain dinginess Gy Waldron wanted to create throughout the film. The biggest challenge in filming this particular sequence came in the timing of the stunt work. Jerry Rushing was the driver who stood in for Bobby Lee to complete the stunt. In the photograph on the next page, you can see that it is Rushing who is climbing out of the door of the car after it has backed into the building.

     When using stunt drivers to complete scenes like this one, the film and action is cut at key intervals. For example, the car is filmed as Rushing backs it into the building, then Rushing climbs out and Kiel Martin gets in the driver's seat to film his lines while the car is in the building. Martin would then step out again, allowing Rushing to take his place behind the wheel and drive the car out of the building safely.

Jerry Rushing climbing out of the driver's seat.
Picture from private collection.

Jerry Rushing proved to be an asset to the crew during the filming of *Moonrunners* not just for his top notch driving skills, but also for his connections. Many of Rushing's friends and family members helped make *Moonrunners* possible. One of those friends was Jim Hogan of Norfolk, Virginia. Hogan first met Rushing after visiting his archery range in Monroe, North Carolina. The two became fast friends, and Rushing turned to Hogan when additional stunt drivers were needed on the *Moonrunners* set.

Rushing, Bill Gribble, and Hogan above. Hogan and wife, Donna, on set at right. *Private Collection.*

Hogan did several bits of stunt driving in the film. One of the more notable pieces is during Bobby Lee's decoy run through town towards the end of the film. Hogan was driving the white Chevrolet pursuing Bobby Lee Hagg. As Hogan rounded a sharp curve in the road, he slid into the ditch bank, putting the car out of commission. Rushing commented "that [it] wasn't supposed to happen that way. Hogan just took that curve too fast." Despite the mistake, the footage was flawless, and production staff elected to keep it in the final cut.

The mistake lends an air of authenticity to the film. Rushing laughingly comments, "not everyone was as good a driver as I was. There were many chases I was involved in that ended like that for the other guy."

"What do you mean there's no indoor plumbing?"

Jesse Hagg farmhouse used in *Moonrunners*.
Picture from private collection.

The house used as Jesse Hagg's home in *Moonrunners* was built in 1868, long before the use of indoor plumbing. As with many older homes, residents would use an "outhouse." Typically built away from the home, an outhouse was often a simple wooden building with a bench style seat situated over a deep hole.

Allen Facemire worked as a camera operator on the film and remembers the education that he received at the hands of the Quicks, the older couple living in the house at the time.

"It was an old monster of a house that had an outhouse out back, which became our honeywagon. The picture didn't have money for mobile dressing rooms or a real honeywagon, so we made use of what was available. When we shot here, that outhouse got ripe fast. You gotta figure with an extra twenty or so people using it, it was guaranteed to smell. Even the old man who lived there complained about it. He quickly taught us the value of using lime after we finished 'our business.' We didn't know any better really; we were all city folk."

Author's Note: A honeywagon is a mobile toilet used primarily in the film industry. Though there is some debate about the origins of the facility's name, many attribute it to the color of the liquid that is pumped out of a honeywagon after it is used. In some cases, these mobile facilities would also be used for wardrobe and makeup.

"I don't know how we did it then."

There is no doubt that technology has developed in the last forty years at break-neck speed. A personal computer was something out of a science fiction novel in 1973, now many people own two or three. Need to reach someone while you're traveling in 1973? Pick up a pay phone and insert a dime; you'll find them at every major gas station and restaurant. Need to reach someone while you're traveling now? Reach in your pocket and pull out your cell phone; you can call anyone anywhere in the world in just a few seconds.

Technology has also changed the motion picture industry significantly in the last forty years. When *Moonrunners* was filmed in 1973, the camera crew used a BNCR lens mount developed by Mitchell Industries for use with a 35 mm movie camera. BNCR actually stands for "Blimped News Camera Reflex," reflecting the practical application of this particular mount in news reporting. It was one of the most highly regarded camera designs of its type and actually serves as a standard by which camera mounts are created today. This particular mount is considered to be one of the most stable, the main reasons it has been preferred for so long.

George Mooradian worked as an assistant cameraman on *Moonrunners* and remembered some of the challenges this particular piece of equipment caused on the set:

"It was incredibly difficult to film chase sequences with the BNCR. You've got to understand that this camera is a pig. It's huge, and it's not easy to maneuver. It's amazing to me that we were able to shoot what we did with this thing. Now, a lot of that stuff is done on handheld with stabilizers, and it's a hundred times easier to capture. The only handhelds that were around back then had really poor quality, so this was really one of our only options."

Echoing Mooradian's comments, Brian Roy recalled being particularly worried about the camera while filming interior shots at the Hagg farmhouse: "My first concern was whether the floors would support the weight of our dolly plus the BNCR."

Sean Doyle, camera operator, with Jim Latham, key grip,
on set with the BNCR camera.
Picture from private collection.

"Of course it's real!"

Jerry Rushing not only gave his life story to Gy Waldron for the film's script, he also served as a technical advisor on the film, assisting the crew in capturing the very essence of a moonshining family. Part of his advisement included making sure props, such as the two (one real, one fake) stills used in the film, were as authentic as possible. The still used to shoot the scene below where Jesse Hagg departs information about his operation to Beth Ann Eubanks couldn't have been more authentic!

Rushing's personal still.
Picture from private collection.

"When it was time to film this scene with Jesse, Bobby Lee, and Beth, we needed a still in the barn, and didn't have one on set. We didn't even have the materials on set to build one." Rushing recalls offering to "[drive] home and pick up one of my stills for the scene. It was currently being used by Uncle Worley, and I could smell the strawberry mash in the cooker as I hauled it back to Georgia from North Carolina."

Rushing picked up the still and got it set up in the barn for the scene without incident. Word that a "real still" was on set managed to leak out to local ATF agents. "As the crew worked to keep the ATF off set, I backed a van up to the barn when the cameras finished rolling and loaded the still into the back. After it was loaded and the scene wrapped, I high tailed it back home just as quick as I could," remarked Rushing. "Those ATF agents were none the wiser," he laughs.

From record labels to peeling labels

Musician Spanky McFarlane of Spanky and Our Gang received a bit part in the film thanks to her relationship with leading man Kiel Martin. Martin was the godfather of Spanky's children and encouraged the casting agency to hire her. She was cast as Precious, the manager of Jake Rainey's bar, and remembers enthusiastically how much fun it was to be on the set: "Everyone was just so nice; it was an absolute blast."

Spanky on set with Rushing.
Picture from Private Collection.

"Sit still!"

Haralson was no stranger to film crews by the time *Moonrunners* wrapped in the area. For the next fifteen or so years, the town played host to numerous production companies as they set up camp in town to capture the "unpolluted South." *Moonrunners* was a first for most of the locals though, and many wanted to claim a piece of the glitz and glamour of Hollywood for themselves. Then there were others who couldn't wait for the crew to leave so that their lives could return to normal.

Local land owner George Boyd rented out some of his property to the crew to use for chase scenes in the movie. Another local land owner, Bill Estes, allowed the crew to film on several of his properties, one of which was the farmhouse featured in the film. Both Boyd and Estes's son-in-law, Frank Wilkinson, remember the thrill the tenant of the farmhouse got from having his home show on the big screen. The tenant, Mr. Quick, was even invited to participate in one of the scenes.

Boyd pointed out that Quick was "the old man sitting beside Jesse on the steps during his checker game with the preacher. The director told Quick to sit beside Jesse and be still. I think he even told the old man not to move or speak." Boyd laughs now thinking back on how still Quick sat in that scene: "It almost looks like they embalmed the man or at least scared him half to death. I don't think he even blinks his eyes!"

Wilkinson remembers that Estes allowed "Mr. Quick to keep the money they gave him to rent the house." Quick got another chance to claim his house was famous several years later when *Driving Miss Daisy* came through town, and the house was featured on film again for a few seconds. Wilkinson stated that "Mr. Quick thoroughly enjoyed each visit the movie people made to Haralson."

"Help! Beauregard!"

Before he was Cooter Davenport on *The Dukes of Hazzard*, local actor Ben Jones often auditioned for bit parts in films as they passed through the Atlanta area. Between these gigs and his appearances in the local theater, Jones quickly carved out a name for himself as a talented actor. Jones learned of *Moonrunners* from pal, Pete Munro, another established Atlantian actor. He was granted the role of Fred, a rookie revenue agent from Chicago.

As Fred, Jones was involved in the bust on the Hagg family still. He was the agent who inquired about arresting and tagging the Haggs's mule, Beauregard. The chief agent, played by Bill Moses, stepped in and rescued Beauregard from Fred, quipping "folks would love to see [agents] follow a mule all summer."

Jones remembers, however, that before Beauregard was 'rescued,' he had to be a *rescuer*. While setting up to film that morning at the creek, the Jeep being used to transport the camera got stuck in the muddy water. Not knowing what to do and desperately needing their equipment, a quick-thinking crew member tied a rope around the Jeep's bumper and looped the other end around the mule. Instinct kicked in, and the mule was able to pull the Jeep free.

According to Jones, he met Jerry Rushing for the first time while the mule was working to break the Jeep free. The two would later be reunited on the set of *The Dukes of Hazzard* in 1978 while filming the episode "Repo Men."

Sometimes real "horse" power is the only thing that will work!
Picture from private collection.

"Go Long!"

Though Jones was only on the set for one day, he had some prime opportunities to bond with the other cast members while set up was going on. Jones remembers sitting around with Jim Mitchum (Grady) and Kiel Martin (Bobby Lee) watching the prop master construct the still with the help of Jerry Rushing. The trio bonded pretty quickly and before long were tossing around a football some- one found. Though their meeting was brief, Jones remembers Mitchum and Martin as a "couple of really nice guys."

Ben Jones on set with Beauregard and Atlanta actor Bill Moses.
Picture from private collection.

Caught redhanded.

One of the fastest ways for a moonshiner to go down is to take pictures of his still as if it were a trophy. It is even worse for a producer if they are also in the shot. Jerry Rushing was always leary about photographic evidence surfacing, and he was careful not to let images get into the wrong hands. The only time Rushing was ever busted for shine was when a photograph of him working surfaced. On set with *Moonrunners*, he had to put aside some of his uneasiness. Despite knowing that the still wasn't real, Rushing still remembers being a little bit jumpy having his picture taken by it.

Jerry Rushing, center, assisting with the
construction of a still for *Moonrunners*.
Picture from private collection.

"A big fish in a little pond."

Many aspects of Rushing's life made it to the silver screen (and the small screen) through Waldron's writing. A principle character in both *Moonrunners* and *The Dukes of Hazzard* was based on a man Rushing knew in Union County: Juke Brooks. Rushing calls Brooks "a big fish in a little pond." He explains, "he was the fella that Waldron used for Jake Rainey and Boss Hogg. He had his hands in everything in Union County, most of it illegal."

Brooks was involved in the liquor business and operated a bar in town that many liquor men frequented. He was a man who appreciated the feel of money in his wallet and the notoriety he earned in his hometown. When Bob Clark began to seek investors for

Moonrunners, surprisingly, Brooks was one of the first in line. His investment, however, came with stipulations.

Brooks was willing to contribute to the film and production company for fifteen minutes of fame. The film, however, was already cast; there was no room left for Brooks. Clark felt the draw of the money and encouraged Waldron to find a place for him. Eventually, it was decided that Brooks would have a very small role. When Bobby Lee and Grady are working the still in the film, there is a tight shot on a pair of hands holding a glass jug at the still's spout. Those are the hands of Juke Brooks. This three second clip was filmed in Monroe on Jerry's property using an operating still (and yes, that is really moonshine). Brooks was content with his cameo and stroked Clark a check.

"Climbing trees ain't all that fun."

Since *Moonrunners* was a low budget film, having the necessary equipment became a problem for director of photography Brian Roy more than once. Though the crew was able to hire a helicopter to film a few shots in the movie, they often had to rely on their own ingenuity to get some of their aerials. Roy explains that in order "to

get the shot [he] needed of Zeebo's car bursting through the bridge roadblock, a tree became [his] new best friend." He further comments: "Waldron and I climbed a tree near the bridge in order to get the camera high enough to capture the entire scene. We learned quickly that Mother Nature was one of the best resources available, and, best of all, she was completely free!"

Roy and Waldron in a tree with the camera.
Picture from private collection.

"Not your average picture car."

Typically, a second unit director and camera operator will use a picture car to get the best possible shots of car action. These picture cars are rigged to pull star cars behind them or even drive directly beside the vehicle being filmed. The camera is given a stable ride, and action is captured on film. *Moonrunners* had one picture car: an old Ford van. The funny thing about this car was that it was never meant to be a picture car; it was primarily used for storage and equipment transportation.

Brian Roy stands atop the crew's "picture car."
Picture from private collection.

Assistant cameraman Bruce MacCallum laughs as he remembers this versatile vehicle: "[That] car was used as a picture car to capture just about every driving shot in the movie. Come to think of it, it was used for everything: a picture car; a storage unit for cameras; even ladders were stored on top of it." Sound mixer Jim Hawkins also remembers the legendary van: "He had *everything* you could possibly need for filming in that van!" Hawkins was referring to Jim Latham, the film's key grip.

Now, no production company would even consider using one vehicle for all of those things, much less using a standard van as a picture car.

"Wait! We are filming a movie on that road!"

Jerry Rushing performed a lot of the stunt driving in *Moonrunners*; considering his long resume as a moonshine hauler and a racecar driver, the leap to stunt driver was not all that unusual. There were some unique challenges, however, that Rushing had never really experienced on either the race track or the back roads of Union County. There is one event in particular that really sticks out in Rushing's mind. It occurred while Rushing was filming a chase sequence with Jerry Randall through Haralson's downtown area. Rushing explains:

"When we were filming the part where Bobby Lee was chased through the town by both Jake's men and the police, the local law enforcement actually helped out by blocking off the roadways so we could shoot without worrying about killing anyone. When I was coming around the corner to slide into the other car, a truck appeared out of no where. I tried turning the wheel to miss him, but I still ended up clipping the front fender at about 50 miles per hour. We found out later that it was a local resident who had slipped past the police block."

Unlike some films which show relatively no body damage to cars, *Moonrunners* allows viewers to see what cars look like after a chase. Rushing notes: "if you look closely you can see the damage done to the car I was driving by the truck. In the film, the driver's side of the car is never hit, but there is clear body damage on screen."

Jerry Randall driving into Rushing's side.
Picture from private collection.

"Are there snakes in that pond?"

Jerry Randall was virtually fearless. The man would jump into a car and do just about anything, unless of course it had to do with snakes. Brian Roy remembers Randall expressing serious concern about snakes before filming a stunt that required him to drive a car into a creek and swim to shore. Randall was nervous enough that another stunt man was even asked to complete the scene for him. Mike Head, who owned Grady's racecar Traveler, remembers being asked to drive the revenuer's car into the creek. Though snakes didn't bother Head, he flatly refused because he couldn't swim. The task fell back to Randall.

"Before Jerry would drive the car off the bridge into the creek," recalls Roy, "we had to check the creek bed area for snakes. It was late September, and the threat for snakes, especially water moccasins, was pretty high. We all searched around for a bit, and found no signs of any reptiles."

That was enough for Randall, who, as Roy remembers, then hopped in the car and drove it right off the side of the bridge, performing a dive into the water and gallantly swimming to shore.

Jerry Randall shaking Brian Roy's hand after the stunt as
Gy Waldron looks on.
Picture from private collection.

"More than just fish in my creek."

George Boyd remembers the day the crew filmed Randall's creek scene, but for an entirely different reason.

"I was returning home from work that evening, when I saw that there was more than fish in my creek. As I drove over the bridge, I could see the back half of a blue car sticking up out of the water," recollects Boyd. "The thing that really got me was they did it without even asking," he shakes his head. "I guess that's Hollywood for you."

Boyd, a local landowner, allowed the production company to rent several pieces of his property for car chases and other miscellaneous scenes. This particular incident soured his relationship with the company primarily because they had not been forthright in explaining to him the condition in which they would be leaving his property.

Actors used live ammunition.
Picture from private collection.

As a low budget production being filmed in rural Georgia, *Moonrunners* did not have some of the red tape to deal with that many other studios encountered both then and now. While this does have definite advantages, there are also some drawbacks. For example, the safety of the cast and crew, while a primary concern, is sometimes jeopardized to create a more realistic scene. These unorthodox practices did not lead to any major injuries on set, however, they certainly could have.

"The interior footage of the Hagg boys and Zeebo shooting the boxes and jugs of liquor was extremely dangerous to capture on film," remarks Brian Roy. "The cast had been sipping on some of Rushing's moonshine all day and were pretty drunk before we even began rolling. Today in the business, actors wouldn't even be allowed to handle loaded weapons, much less shoot them in front of cameras, and they certainly wouldn't be allowed to do it while intoxicated. We didn't really care that much back then, I guess." Roy expands, "Jim [Mitchum] was shooting really close to my camera, and I was starting to get a little antsy. As my anxiety rose, the shooting became more and more outrageous. All of a sudden, a piece of buckshot ricocheted off of something in the gin and caught me in the forehead."

Roy was thankful "it didn't break the skin," but he remembers that it was incredibly painful. "That's exactly why we have the rules we do today," he adds.

"Now that's a blast from the past."

Williamson resident Faye Patton has lived in the area for most of her life. Like many other locals, she knows the ins and outs of her small town as if they were the ins and outs of her own life. Given the unusual appearance of a production company in her town, Patton took note of the men and their work. "It was hard not to," she commented, "they kind of stuck out like sore thumbs."

The most exciting memory Patton has of Waldron and his crew pertains to the cotton gin explosion at the conclusion of the film. She explains:

"That was a long time ago, but it sticks out in my mind like it was yesterday. The whole neighborhood was excited about it. They were supposed to blow it up around eleven o'clock at night, but things kept getting pushed back, and it ended up happening around four in the morning. Some of my neighbors sat on their roofs, while others looked out windows. It seemed like it was taking forever for them to get it done. When they finally blew it up, it was definitely worth the wait. I've never seen anything so powerful in my life. Some of my neighbors even had windows blown out by it!"

"You're going to stand where?"

The crew received permission from W.C. Adamson of Williamson to blow up a portion of his cotton gin. In preparation, special effects coordinator Bob Shelley spent an entire day lining the interior of the gin with primer cord and black powder. He wanted to make sure the explosion was a good one, just as Adamson wanted to make sure the building was gone.

While preparing to film the scene, Allen Facemire and Tom Skarda rigged a temporary shelter for the camera and positioned themselves fairly close to the building. As Facemire was measuring for the shot, he noticed that Shelley was considerably further away from the building than he was. Facemire asked Shelley about his location and then asked about where his camera was positioned. Shelley looked at Facemire and asked, "do you see that hill over there?" Facemire responded with "yes," noticing that the hill was about a quarter of a mile from the building. Shelley said, "That's where I'll be."

Facemire looked back at the shelter he'd built for the camera. He knew that was ultimately the best angle for the shot, so he decided to stay put despite Shelley's warning. Everything was a go, and Facemire got into position and began rolling film. When the building exploded, the force was so great that the camera was pushed backwards into Facemire, and the shelter was significantly damaged. Facemire laughs today as he recalls that moment: "I got a black eye, but that shot was perfect."

"I blew up your still."

Bob Shelley got his break into the film industry with *Moon-runners*. He was hired to take care of some of the special effects on the film, including the still explosion and the concluding gin explosion. Prior to his work in the motion picture industry, Shelley actually worked for the Alcohol, Tobacco, and Firearms (ATF) division of the federal government. Shelley was part of the crew that came in after a still had been captured to destroy it. He learned a great deal about explosives on his job, which is what set him on the pathway to special effects work.

After getting the *Moonrunners* job, Shelley was certain he had heard the name Rushing before. It didn't take him long to realize that he'd heard it in his former life as an ATF explosives expert. In the late 1960s, Shelley was working in Southern North Carolina. He was called into the Union County area to destroy a large still that had been captured recently. The still belonged to Jerry Rushing.

During filming, Shelley remembers meeting Rushing on set. He explained:

"I walked over to Jerry and said, 'You won't remember me, but back a few years ago I was working around Monroe with the ATF. I actually helped them blow up one of your stills.' Rushing started laughing, which surprised me, but I was really thankful he had a good attitude about the whole thing. It just goes to show you what a small world it really is."

For Rushing, this story was really just representative of the relationships he'd seen between moonshiners and revenuers. "There was never any doubt between us that we all just wanted to do our jobs. We may have hated each other, but we didn't really hold it against the person," he continues, "it was more or less the position that we didn't like."

"Going Bananas"

The crew takes a quick snack break.
Picture from private collection.

During the filming of most productions, cast and crew are fed and generally cared for by craft service. Craft service is primarily responsible for cordoning off the set area and making sure that food and drink are available throughout the day for those working on the set. The food available for the cast and crew varies greatly depending on the type of production. For *Moonrunners*, there was no craft services department. Those working on the set were responsible for bringing in their own food each day. Many of the crew members recall grabbing food from the hotel before leaving for the set or stopping while on the way out of Griffin.

In the photograph on the previous page, several crew members can be seen snacking on bananas. There are also several watermelons stacked on the ground. Brian Roy commented that this photo was taken as a "joke because someone had actually brought food for the crew to a location."

Moonrunners: Deleted Scenes

Like most films, *Moonrunners* went through extensive re-writes both during filming and in post-production. There were several scenes that were cut from the original script prior to cameras rolling on location. And there were a few that were filmed, but removed later during the final edit to cut back on time or create continuity. There were even a few scenes that were removed because the final outcome would have proven too risque for some of the target audiences. Each of these deleted scenes, however, adds a little more color to the story and creates a much richer narrative.

The deleted scenes are described here in the order they appear in the original *Moonrunners* script.

Deleted Scene One: Bobby Lee and Harlan

Bobby Lee talking about his life with another prisoner.
Picture from private collection.

The period of time when Bobby Lee is in jail is expanded in Waldron's initial draft of the script. While the actual sentence of thirty days was adhered to, the original script includes many sequences which would have provided the audience with a richer understanding of Bobby Lee Hagg.

To start with, the original script expands upon one of the most confusing issues of continuity in the film: Bobby Lee's guitar. When the film starts, Bobby Lee pulls up to the Boar's Nest with Grady in anticipation of playing with the band. Things go badly for him, however, when he assaults a patron in the bar with his guitar, smashing the instrument into pieces. He is then arrested by the Pickens County officers, and, presumably, he is sentenced immediately. When he is released from jail, however, it is impossible not to notice that he climbs out of the officer's car at the "county line" with a perfectly intact guitar.

What producers cut from the film was the story of how Bobby Lee came to possess this second guitar, leaving viewers with some confusion. The sequence as Waldron wrote it has Bobby Lee befriending a fellow "jail bird" and learning the ins and outs of the Pickens County Jail. His "education" culminates with the event that gained him possession of "Harlan," the guitar.

In the photograph on the previous page, Bobby Lee can be seen scrubbing the floor with his new friend. As they work, a deputy, Clifford, walks up behind the two men and grins. After he walks away, the other prisoner explains to Bobby Lee part of the social hierarchy they are operating under: "You better watch yourself, man. He likes 'em pretty, like you." Though startled by this information, Bobby Lee appears to not be bothered by the deputy's actions and preferences. At nearly the end of his prison sentence, he has another encounter with Clifford when another prisoner is brought into his cell.

Clifford brings a wet, drunken derelict into Bobby Lee's cell and tosses him on the other bed. The man is obviously shivering and appears to be quite ill. Bobby Lee expresses concern about the man's condition to Clifford and is met without sympathy. Clifford even goes as far as challenging Bobby Lee to "curl up next to him and keep him nice an' warm." He then further antagonizes Bobby Lee by saying that the man is Bobby Lee's "type." Bobby Lee challenges Clifford's accusation, only to have Clifford mock his musical ability by holding up the man's beaten up guitar and proclaim that it "looks like we're gonna be ass-deep in culture around here."

Bobby Lee is more interested in the old man's well being than in Clifford's remarks. While Clifford mutters about the man, stating that his name is Gerald Hemmings, Lee covers the man with a blanket and removes his wet shirt. As he's doing this, Bobby Lee discovers a leather pouch with old newspaper clippings in it and realizes the man was the popular song writer Harlan Hemmings. Excited by his discovery, Bobby Lee tries to vigorously rouse the man from his stupor, but it is no use, the man dies.

Bobby Lee informs Clifford of the man's death and tries to tell him who the man was. Clifford provides the audience with no recognition and the man with no sympathy. As Clifford makes arrangements to have the body removed, Bobby Lee casually asks what will happen to the man's guitar. Clifford blandly explains that it will be sold at the sheriff's auction. After a brief exchange wherein he taunts Bobby Lee with the instrument, Clifford finally says, "looks like you're not gonna get this fine guitar." Bobby Lee is visibly upset and turns away from the antagonistic guard. After prolonged silence, Clifford finally asks Bobby Lee if he "really wants it," and Bobby Lee simply nods. With a simple "how bad?" and a "chilling smile" from Clifford, viewers are left to imagine the exchange that took place.

The next scene was described by Waldron as follows: "Sound of guitar softly strumming - reveals Lee sitting on his bed softly playing guitar." It's the morning that Bobby Lee gets out of jail. As he gets his personal items back and accounts that everything is there, Clifford holds up a guitar pick and viciously grins: "You want to try for his pick?" Bobby Lee squares up to Clifford and responds, "No. I'll rough it," and he heads out to find his ride.

Aside from this exchange that occurs while Bobby Lee is in jail, Waldron also included a bit of Jerry Rushing's personal history in this deleted sequence. When Bobby Lee first arrives and starts to converse with the other prisoners, the topic of former sentences is broached. When Bobby Lee is asked if he's been in jail before, he responds that he "did a year in State Pen when [he] was seventeen." The other prisoner asks if Bobby Lee's sentence was because of liquor, but Bobby Lee informs him that it was not:

Milk. Me and some boys broke into the high school one night. That's all there was to steal. Milk. I came up before a judge who'd been trying to nail my daddy for liquor, and he never could. So he got me. Three years. State prison. For milk. My daddy had never let me haul before that. Boy, I swore if I ever got locked up again, it was gonna be for haulin' liquor.

Waldron's inclusion of this particular anecdote is directly out of Rushing's story. Prior to a conviction later in life, the only sentence Rushing served in the state penitentiary was over a half pint of milk. The story is quite similar to the one that Waldron gives to Bobby Lee. Rushing was with a group of boys one summer who decided to break into the local high school. While inside, they went to the cafeteria in search of food only to find milk being stored. Rushing consumed a half a pint of milk while on the property; another member of his party stole a few pints. All of the boys were caught by a local law enforcement officer.

When Rushing went before the judge in his trial, he was sentenced to eight months in the state penitentiary, serving as a model to the rest of the Rushing family. The judge, who had never been able to give any Rushing a sentence for moonshine, wanted to make an example about of Jerry's behavior to demonstrate the power held by the local courts. This fueled a deep hatred within Rushing regarding the corruption of local government officials.

Deleted Scene Two: The Haggs Strike Back

The repainted Traveler being prepped for this scene.
Picture from private collection.

After Jake asks Jesse to join up with him again to supply the syndicate and Jesse refuses, Jake calls a war against the Haggs. He threatens the family business by promising to drive anyone off the road who is delivering Jesse's liquor and by blowing up any Hagg still they come across in the woods. Jesse takes Jake's words with a grain of salt, but the boys are out for blood.

In a scene that was deleted from the film to conserve time, Bobby Lee and Grady are at the garage painting Traveler. The Balladeer explains: "Since Jake Rainey had declared war - Lee and Grady decided to take the offensive. But they didn't tell Jesse anything about it. He'd worry." The boys planned to attack anyone who was making deliveries to Jake's truck stop, however, when the moment came to make a final decision about their target, it was an easy choice for Grady: "Cooter Fairchild was the one that caused Grady to lose that last stock car race. Cooter figured he was about the hottest thing on wheels. So Lee and Grady decided to help him prove it."

Bobby Lee and Grady repaint Traveler a white-gray color and wait in the woods near Cooter's home on a night they know he is planning to deliver to Jake. The only thing the Hagg boys didn't know was that two Federal agents were also staked out that night waiting for Cooter to make his run. As Cooter exits his place, Bobby Lee and Grady pull out behind him. The two cars enter into a high speed chase, which, as The Balladeer puts it, "weren't much of a chase - Cooter had a heavy load of 120 proof liquor and the boys had Traveler."

As Bobby Lee pulls up beside Cooter's car, Grady lights a fire arrow and fires right into Cooter's rear window. The flaming arrow crashes through the jugs in the back. Without a pause, Grady leans out of Traveler and fires again. The camera flashes to a shot of Cooter's face, and he appears terrified as he realizes the liquor in the back of his car has caught on fire. Bobby Lee backs off Cooter's bumper, allowing him to pull in front. As he attempts to escape, Grady lights one more arrow and fires it into the back of the car just as the duo is passing the ATF car.

The agents are stunned by what they are seeing. Fred, played by Ben Jones in the released film, looks at his partner and asks, "Are you people still having Indian trouble?" The two agents laugh and pull out to join in the chase. As Bobby Lee looks in his rearview and sees the flashing lights of the agents' car, he smiles: "Federal. And me not carrying a single thing illegal." Bobby Lee and Grady laugh and speed ahead of Cooter, who has just run into a ditch and jumped out of his car. As the ATF car approaches, Bobby Lee completes a "bootlegger's turn" and comes charging back toward them. The ATF car slides in the opposite ditch as Bobby Lee speeds between the two, and Cooter's car explodes.

The following scene is at the Pettigrew brothers' still, which is included in the final cut of the film. The more interesting note to this particular deleted scene is that all of the action—typically the most expensive part of any production—was filmed. The arrows were fired. The car was blown up. The stunt men were paid for their time. And yet, it was still not included in the final edit.

This scene was the first footage filmed when the crews arrived in Haralson, Georgia. According to a shooting schedule, this was shot on Monday, September 17, the first official day of filming. The stunt was completed by Georgia short track driver Charlie Mincey, Traveler's real owner, Mike Head, and Jerry Rushing. Mincey drove the car, while Head rode shogtun, and Rushing fired arrows out of Traveler's side windows.

Deleted Scene Three: The Boar Hunt

To capitalize on one of Jerry Rushing's sayings, Waldron should have known that "you can't train a wild boar." As an experienced hunter and trapper, Rushing has seen more than his fair share of attacks from wild boar. They are small, vicious animals whose tusks can easily rip into the skin of any animal or human it encounters. Now, imagine trying to film a boar hunting scene. It's not only unrealistic, it's down right stupid. Wild boar are unpredictable when they feel threatened, and to place a cameraman in a boar's path to get the right footage would surely have resulted in major catastrophe. Aside from the difficulty of filming with wild animals, the scene is also quite long, following the progress of several of hunting parties and yet another romantic encounter. This, however, is exactly what Gy Waldron wanted to do as a precursor to Jake's big barbecue.

Hunting was and is a huge part of Southern culture, especially for families living in rural areas. For many families, hunting was a major part of supplying a family with meat, which is how Jerry Rushing got his start in the sport. The same went for Waldron's

Hagg family. Grady and Bobby Lee were avid hunters, both for practical reasons and pleasure. As it was written into the beginning of the film, both were forced to hunt with bows as they were on probation and couldn't own guns. The same was true for Rushing; his start as a bow hunter came from abiding by the requirements of his probation. Soon the bow that was forced on him became a love and a talent; Rushing had a successful run as a competitive archer, as did his wife, Dean.

The boar hunt Waldron wrote into the script was a big one. As Waylon Jennings narrates: "[The boys] wouldn't have missed Jake's hunt anyway - regardless of the war with Jake. Them boys would have gone hunting on Judgment Day with the devil himself - if it was gonna be a good hunt. And this was gonna be a good 'un. You could feel it in the air. The kind of hunt you lie about for years to come." The hunt was divided up in to teams; Bobby Lee and Grady were teamed up with Charlie, a character who did not make the final cut. Competing against the cousins and their friend, were the Pettigrew brothers and Cooter, Zeebo and Blackie, and several other groups of Jake's liquor men.

The excitement of the hunt was built by lots of good natured banter between the teams and Charlie's nerves about participating in his first boar hunt. Without a great deal of dialogue, Waldron describes several camera shots that would have been set to music. The men were hunting with dogs, and there were several clips of the dogs catching the scent of a boar and leading the chase. Bobby Lee and Grady break the crest of a hill after the dogs only to "come up on [two] girls who was out berry pickin'. Except there wasn't any berries around there." Just as soon as Grady saw the girls, he began "licking his chops" in anticipation. After one of the girls slides off into the bushes, Grady makes to follow her, but Bobby Lee stops him: "Hey - we huntin' or whorin'?" Bobby Lee's admonition doesn't have any long lasting affect on Grady, who simply shrugs his shoulders and heads off into the bushes after his new lady.

As Bobby Lee watches the bushes where Grady disappeared, a boar runs into his line of sight, and The Balladeer comments, "It was at that moment in his life that Bobby Lee realized how much hunting really meant to him." Bobby Lee takes off after the boar and leaves Grady behind. He quickly finds Charlie, who is hot on the trail of one of the boars.

The camera then pans to Zeebo and Blackie as they follow the trail of the hog they spotted earlier. The two follow the dogs to a thicket of bushes where they hear the occasional rustle of leaves and animalistic grunt. A coin is flipped to determine who will be the unlucky one to crawl into the brush after the hog. Zeebo loses and heads in only to discover the rustling and grunts belong to Grady and his new friend. The girl takes off, leaving Grady hanging. Having no better alternative, Grady decides to rejoin the hunt and follows Zeebo and Blackie as they pursue their boar.

The story switches back to Bobby Lee and Charlie, who, with the help of dogs, have bayed a boar. Charlie takes his first shot and misses; the boar begins to get angry, and Charlie's nerves skyrocket. Bobby Lee tries to coach Charlie: "When you hit him, you go for a tree to one side or the other. They ain't no way you can outrun a boar." This time when Charlie takes aim he hits the boar; the boar, now wounded, heads for a nearby thicket. Bobby Lee tells Charlie that it's time to go after the boar, but Charlie wants nothing more to do with it. He tells Bobby Lee that he "wouldn't go after [it] with a machine gun." His behavior and unwillingness to finish the job frustrate Bobby Lee, who heads after Charlie's wounded boar.

Waldron's explanation of a wounded boar's behavior is dead on accurate; The Balladeer narrates as Bobby Lee pursues the boar: "The boar, being smart, usually goes for the roughest country he can find once he knows you're after him. Then, when he wears you down, he's very likely to go into a thicket and wait for you. And that's just what this one did." Bobby Lee pursues the boar into a dense thicket; he tracks the animal cautiously and quietly, looking for any indication that it will charge. Suddenly, the animal charges Bobby Lee, leaving the thicket and chasing him down to a nearby creek. Bobby Lee rushes into the water, assuming the boar will not follow. Just as he hits the creek, Grady and Zeebo come over the crest of a nearby ridge.

Grady, acting on instinct, draws his bow back and prepares to shoot the boar that has Bobby Lee trapped. He's stopped, however, by Bobby Lee, who insists that he is going to be the one to take this boar out. He asks for Grady to toss him an arrow and a bow. He lines up his shot and fires. The scene is written to immediately cut to a shot of the boar roasting over a fire at Jake's barbecue.

The hunt was cut, as stated previously, because of its unrealistic nature. There would be no way to film the scene in the manner that Waldron prescribed in his script. The work would simply be too dangerous for actors, stunt men, and crew, and any attempt to film a hunt without actually having it would seem contrived on film, causing the moment to lose its authenticity.

Deleted Scene Four: Reba's Secrets

Between the beginning of Jake's barbecue festivities and Jake's talk with Bobby Lee, there was a deleted exchange between Jake and one of the other liquor men. During the party, Jake is seen with his arm around one of the girls in attendance. One of the men is quick to speak up that Jake "better not let Reba catch him with his arm around another woman." The other men laugh, but Jake knows he is safe. He responds, "Reba hates barbecue so she stayed at home. Besides, she doesn't like to come around other women; she hates competition." The knowledge that no other woman could really compete with Reba's beauty doesn't keep the men from enjoying Jake's little quip about his lovely wife.

This comment isn't lost on another party-goer, who immediately disappears from the site. Grady, who'd been listening to Jake's comments and watching Jake during the party, took leave from the scene just as soon as he heard that Reba was at home alone. He figured that he would have just enough time to steal Jesse's liquor back from Jake and visit Reba before anyone, especially Jake, noticed he was gone. Waldron cut this scene as it was a precursor to another (longer) deleted sequence that happened after Jake spoke with Bobby Lee and left his own party.

The deleted sequence began with non-verbal communication between Bobby Lee and Grady in which Grady lets Bobby Lee know he's slipping out. The cousins had prearranged the strike on Jake's truck stop to retrieve their liquor. The plan was for one of them to sneak over there during the barbecue when the place would be unattended. After Grady sneaks off, Jake heads to leave his party and Bobby Lee intercepts him; this scene is left in the film. Bobby Lee is largely satisfied because he knows that Jake's house is well in the opposite direction of his truck stop, and if Jake is there, nothing should bother Grady on his run.

The problem with this is Bobby Lee isn't thinking like Grady. After successfully getting the liquor from Jake's, Grady heads over to Jake's house for a quick "visit" with Reba. When his pickup pulls up in front of the house, Reba comes out on the porch and leans against a support post. Just as Grady steps out of the truck and heads over to his girl, Jake surprises both Reba and Grady by popping out from behind a tree with a shotgun. Reba screams, "Jake!" Grady turns just in time to see Jake raise his gun and fire the first shot.

Grady dives out of the way of Jake's buckshot, and the pellets blast the truck window and door; he begins to run towards the woods. Jake follows, still shooting, and screams, "I knew you'd show - you son of a bitch!" As Jake follows Grady to the woods, firing and reloading all the way, Reba stands on the porch watching the chase in restrained amazement. Once she is assured both men are well occupied and far enough away for comfort, Reba sneaks around to the back of the house and opens the door of a small shed. "All clear," she whispers, and Precious, Jake's truck stop manager (played by singer Spanky McFarlane), peers around the shed door.

Reba explains to her that it "was Grady's truck [they] heard drive up. Then Jake [popped] out from behind a tree and [started] shooting." Precious nods in understanding as Reba continues, "I wish you could get Jake to take you out a few times - Then if he ever finds out about us - he won't be able to say nothing." Precious obviously shares Reba's sentiment, and in an effort to maintain their secret, sneaks back to the truck stop before Jake sees her.

It is likely that this scene was not just edited out for time. The addition of such a racy, sexual suggestion would likely not have appealed to the targeted market of Southern conservatives. Just as with Bobby Lee's suggestive dealings with Clifford the Pickens County deputy, Reba's closeted relationship with Precious sends the film's overall 'harmless' image flying out the door. In order to draw a larger audience at screenings, the film was tailored to be gritty, but reserved.

Deleted Scene Five: Sores on a Jackass

Following his encounter with Jake, Grady has more than one battle wound that needs to be tended. Jesse digs buckshot out of Grady's rear while Bobby Lee watches with great interest. Jesse, as usual, is in the dark about the details surrounding Grady's injury and tries to keep up with the boys' conversation.

Jesse treating Grady's wound.
Picture from private collection.

Grady is mad at Bobby Lee because he was under the impression Lee would make sure that Jake was where he needed to be. Bobby Lee is frustrated with Grady's womanizing, but amused by the present situation. He says: "[Jake] went home. I figured that was the safest place - since you was supposed to be at his truck stop stealing back our liquor. How was I supposed to know you was at his house after his wife? And you ended up not getting either one."

As Jesse is starting to put two and two together, Beth comes in with a bottle of turpentine. Figuring the best way to get through to Grady would be by making him holler, Jesse comments, "[this] is the best thing there is for curing sores on a jackass. Ought to work just fine, here." He then begins to apply the liquid liberally to Grady's wounds, and his point is made: Grady begins to shriek as the turpentine does its work.

Deleted Scene Six: A Happy Ending?

Waldron's initial ending for *Moonrunners* is not the devastation at Jake's cotton gin that we see as the credits begin to roll on screen today. After Bobby Lee and Grady make the final deal with Jake, Bobby Lee drives off into the 'sunset' with Beth; the couple plans to make their way to Nashville, where they are "gonna be stars." In the final cut, we simply see the two drive off in Beth's car (which is, ironically, red again rather than yellow); however, Waldron's initial script has the cameras following Bobby Lee and Beth as they hit the road.

A bit out of town, the camera stops on the couple sitting in the car on the side of the road. As it moves to the interior, Bobby Lee says, "Jesse once said that about the dumbest thing a woman can do is get pregnant when she don't want to, and the dumbest thing a man can do is run out of gas." Bobby Lee looks over at Beth: "You ain't pregnant, are you?" She quickly responds that she is not. He then adds, "well, I have sure as hell run out of gas." The two slowly climb out of the car and start walking down the road holding hands.

A car approaches them from behind, and Bobby Lee sticks out his thumb for a ride. He smiles in an attempt to charm the driver into giving them a lift, but notices that Beth is not smiling at all. The man driving the car looks at both of them. Beth turns to Bobby Lee: "Lee... This is my stepdaddy." Bobby Lee is stunned, and Beth Ann's stepdaddy is not amused at her choice in company. "Bethel Ann Eubanks - Get in the car. You, too, boy," he barks at them. Bobby Lee starts to take off running, but Beth Ann grabs his hand and drags him with her, "No, Daddy, I can explain. Y'see...." She trails off as the car speeds away, and the credits begin to roll on screen.

While it is tempting to wrap up the film in such a clever way, the ending is then left too open to speculation. Additionally, the step-father angle was largely dropped after Beth Ann explained to Jesse why she ran away from home. His words on the matter, "Ain't your Pa heard there ain't no more slavery," ended any possibility of Beth Ann returning to her family. To end both Beth Ann and Bobby Lee's dreams and force them into the hands of such a predator would take away the sense of triumph audiences feel when Bobby Lee and Grady finally trump Jake. In the editing room, producers elected to cut this particular clip wisely. Concluding the film with Jake's demise, Bobby Lee and Grady's triumph, and Beth Ann and Bobby Lee's departure for Nashville accurately portrays the feeling that, in the end, it's always the good ol' boys who win.

Moonrunners: The Cars

To keep production costs as low as possible, Bob Clark, the film's producer, elected to purchase many of the cars at auction. The end result was the acquisition of many retired police cars and taxis, all of which were less than three years old. Gy Waldron wanted to make sure that the stunts were as realistic as possible. He also wanted to make sure that the cars showed realistic damage. Unlike the magical power the General Lee possessed in *The Dukes of Hazzard*, the cars used in filming *Moonrunners* definitely showed their battle wounds. Dings and dents followed the cars throughout the film, adding to the authenticity of Waldron's colorful story.

Bobby Lee's Moonrunner is a 1971 Plymouth Fury II.

Jake Rainey drove a 1966 Cadillac DeVille. This was actually Bill Estes's car.

Zeebo drove a 1970 Plymouth Fury.

Beth Ann Eubanks stole her stepdaddy's 1971 Chevrolet Bel Air. This is the yellow car that Jesse was last seen using to haul liquor.

Grady's truck was a 1950 Ford F-1.

Traveler (#54) was a 1955 Chevrolet 210.

The revenue agent (played by Jerry Randall) drove a 1971 Plymouth Fury II.

The Pickens County police car was a 1969 Plymouth Fury.

Jake's men (including Jerry Rushing) and the other Shiloh officers drove 1971 Chevrolets, including the Biscayne model.

Bobby Lee Hagg's 1971 Plymouth Fury II.

Picture from Private Collection.

 *Moonrunners*: Filming Locations

When Gy Waldron and Bob Clark decided to film *Moonrunners*, they knew they would need a location that reflected the rural South. They also knew they would need a location that was near Atlanta—their headquarters and the seat of a burgeoning film industry.

Moonrunners was filmed in the towns of Williamson and Haralson, Georgia. Neither of these places are strangers to the film industry with numerous big-budget Hollywood studios choosing to shoot here because of the picturesque nature of the two towns. Both areas have a long and fascinating history. Both areas have also avoided some of the major development creeping southward from Atlanta.

While not Rushing's native soil of North Carolina, this region of Georgia accurately and adequately reflected the landscape and personality of Union County.

This section focuses on the locations used in filming *Moonrunners*. Due to copyright laws, printing images from the film is prohibited, therefore the pictures shown are of the locations today. Locations are included in sequence.

The cast and crew were housed at the Holiday Inn in Griffin, Georgia during filming. The hotel was one of the finest in the area at that time, boasting a full service restaurant and a pool. It has since switched hands and is now part of the Howard Johnson chain. Not just where the cast and crew laid their heads at night, the hotel also served as the backdrop for a love scene between Reba and Grady in the film. While considerably more developed today, many crew members described Griffin as a one-horse town. In fact, few remember there being anything more than the Holiday Inn and a few mom-and-pop establishments.

The building above was used as the Boar's Nest in the opening sequence of the movie. While it is now a garage, the exterior has largely remained untouched. The photo below shows the interior of the shop. This doorway is where Grady re-enters the room to discover that Bobby Lee has just gotten himself into trouble.

This location is where Beth's car is seen after Bobby Lee backed it into the biker bar. Below is where Bobby Lee falls out of Beth's car, laughing about backing into the bar. This road, Al Roberts Road in Haralson, is in front of the Hagg farmhouse.

West Atlanta Raceway is where Grady raced Traveler. These photographs were taken in 2004, the last year that the speedway was open. In the photo below, you can see the grandstands were largely the same as they appeared in 1973.

Sometime in 2005, West Atlanta Raceway was demolished to make way for a housing development. This picture was taken from the vantage point of the track's back straight away. The destruction of the West Atlanta Raceway is just another example of how much of the South's history is being erased to make way for residential and commercial development.

Above is a picture of Roy Adderholt's barn as it looks today. This is where Bobby Lee and Zeebo start their liquor run after the race. Below is the interior of the barn where the boys load their respective cars with Roy's shine and determine the route they will drive to Jake Rainey's.

When Bobby Lee and Zeebo left Roy's barn, they made Roy call the police with a tip off about their run. The boys did this "to make it interesting." After running off the road at the intersection above, the pair find the resulting road block set up on the road below.

Bobby Lee escapes the road block by driving onto the hillside above. He then drives off into the distance on the road below, heading for Jake's truck stop. This location is actually used again later in the film for another road block. It appears different because it was shot at a different angle.

The location above is where Jake Rainey's truck stop once stood. The truck stop was operated and owned by Ronald Glazier until a few years ago. Glazier closed the truck stop and sold the property. A housing development called "Musick Park" recently broke ground on the location. This is one of the many residential developments creeping southward from Atlanta. This is located approximately two miles North of Haralson.

The house used as the Hagg farmhouse was built in the late nineteenth century and stood as a testament to high Southern Victorian style though it had largely fallen into disrepair by the time *Moonrunners* was filmed. The house burned sometime in 2005 under questionable circumstances. Frank Wilkinson, Mr. Estes's son-in-law, surmises some locals set it ablaze. The steps in the photograph above, along with the two fireplaces, are all that remain. This part of the porch was featured in the film when Jesse Hagg plays checkers with the preacher. The other older gentleman in the shot was Mr. Quick. He was invited by the crew to participate in the scene.

While the undergrowth has made this site nearly unrecogniz-
able, Jerry Rushing confirmed that this creek is where the
Hagg's still was located. Just on the outskirts of Haralson, this
area provided the perfect backdrop for the revenuer bust and
still explosion.

As you look at the circled area, you are actually seeing the farmhouse's ruins. This intersection is featured when Bobby Lee pulls out of the house driveway on a liquor run. The picture below is of the road at the intersection where he turns and drives off with his load.

Bobby Lee is pursued by a revenuer and several police officers during his run. The road above was used in one of the
chase scenes. As they reach the intersection, they swing onto
the road below actually knocking down the stop sign as they
turn.

With the revenue agent still on Bobby Lee's tail, Lee pulls a fast one on the agent coming over the railroad tracks above and making a bootlegger's turn and speeding off to the right. The road below is part of a four way intersection Bobby Lee tried to escape in. He is seen coming down this road before he makes a hard left.

Bobby Lee makes a hard left onto the road above showing off his slick driving skills. Lee then quickly spins around and takes off down the road below, continuing in the direction he was originally headed.

This area is where Bobby Lee pulls into a driveway and runs right into a corn field with a revenuer in hot pursuit during his liquor run. Just behind the trees in the center is a house, which can be seen clearly in the film.

The dam above is part of Elder's Mill. Bobby Lee and Beth walk across the top of the dam into the woods as they are looking for a site for a new still. Below is another view of Jesse Hagg's farmhouse. This angle is seen when Bobby Lee pulls into the driveway with Beth. If you look closely at the photo below, you can see a large support beam resting on the porch steps.

Located in the historic town square of downtown Fayetteville, Georgia, this courthouse was used to introduce Sheriff Roscoe Coltrane in the film. As Coltrane walks down the front steps, the camera pans up and Waylon Jennings narrates.

One of the only locations outside of Haralson, picturesque Williamson served as a focal point in the film when Zeebo lures Bobby Lee and Grady into a race. You can see three men sitting on a bench in front of the store above in the film. The road below is where the two cars pull away and the race begins.

Part of Zeebo's race included Jake's plan to catch Bobby Lee and Grady. Jake had Coltrane set up a roadblock just wide enough for Zeebo to bust through on the bridge above. Rather than follow him, Bobby Lee and Grady pulled onto the dirt road below to escape.

They may have escaped Sheriff Coltrane and his deputies, but Bobby Lee and Grady ended up getting ambushed by Jake's men. This dirt road is actually the road that Bobby Lee turns down in the previous scene. For once the "magic" of Hollywood maintained some continuity in its locations.

As a side note, one of the armed, masked men in the ambush scene was played by Jerry Rushing. Though Jerry was not credited as acting in this film, he portrays Jake Rainey's bodyguard and right hand man in the story.

Local farmer William "Bill" Estes was a major asset to the crew during filming. This location was actually a campground Estes owned. It was featured as the location for Jake's barbeque. The building seen in the film was destroyed by fire years ago, but the landscape has remained virtually the same.

Jake Rainey comes to see Jesse in a last ditch effort to get Jesse into his syndicate deal. The above picture shows what is left of the barn. It was featured in numerous shots, in fact, one of Jesse's stills was located inside. Below is the area where Jake drives up. The Cadillac he is driving belonged to Bill Estes.

Jesse Hagg was a man of principle. He attended church, he took pride in his craft, and he even paid taxes on the corn he grew to make liquor. The above shot is taken from the vantage point used to film Jesse as he explained to the boys that his liquor, like the Model T Ford, is "one of a kind." He thoroughly convinced Bobby Lee and Grady that Jake was not doing the kind of business he wanted to be involved in.

Brian Roy did whatever it took to get the shot, and the above is one of the best. This road, Al Roberts Road, was used to shoot part of the chase sequence when Bobby Lee is driving decoy and Jake's men pull out behind him. The natural, hilly landscape lent a fantastic feel to this particular moment.

This particular four-way intersection is featured during Bobby Lee's decoy run. He pulls around the above corner into the lumber yard below before circling back into town. The attempt to lose Jake's men failed, but he was able to pull ahead of them.

Just as soon as Bobby Lee turns back onto the road from the lumber yard, he smashes into the side of one of Jake's henchmen. The attempt to knock his "enemy" off the road fails and causes some damage to both cars. The above road is just off the intersection and on the way into town.

Coming into town, Bobby Lee turns the corner above with two of Jake's men in pursuit. The white-colored car that turns the corner last (driven by Jim Hogan) takes the curve far too fast and slides into the ditch below. This road, Dead Oak Road, leads directly into the downtown section of Haralson.

As Bobby Lee continues toward town, he rounds this curve with the last remaining of his pursuers tight on his tail. Bobby Lee's Fury was driven by Jerry Randall for all of this stunt work. The pursuing car was driven by Jerry Rushing.

These buildings are part of "downtown" Haralson. They are located near the former Haralson Cotton Gin. Bobby Lee races around the above corner as the pursuing car turns in a different direction to attempt a cut off. As Bobby Lee rounds the corner below, a police car joins in the chase.

These roads are in the same section of town. Jake's man rounds the back of the above building, crossing over to the road below. Bobby Lee has already driven by, so the car turns and heads past the cotton gin on the right in the picture below. The metal building in the photo above was used as Roy Adderholt's barn.

As Bobby Lee runs from Jake's men, he cuts behind the cotton gin on the road above. He may have out maneuvered the other car, but the police car is still close behind. The owner of this once operational gin was Bill Estes. Mr. Estes's son-in-law, Frank Wilkinson, remembers struggling to finish ginning his cotton while the cast and crew were in town filming *Moonrunners*.

Still in pursuit of Bobby Lee, Jake's men drive past the house above. Suddenly, Bobby Lee pulls out onto the below road, colliding into the other car and sending them both sliding down the train tracks. Both cars were badly damaged during this bit of stunt work.

Bobby Lee is caught by the cop after his collision with Jake's hired hands. The above location is where Bobby Lee laughingly explains to the officer that he was actually hauling water, not moonshine. The driveway just past the tracks is also where Beth Ann's car, now yellow, can be seen pulling out. Bobby Lee is riding so high on his success that he doesn't even mind the inconvenience of being ticketed.

The area above is where Grady's truck was parked while he was with Reba in Traveler. Traveler was housed in a garage, which is now a go-cart shop. When Grady realizes he is running late, he quickly leaves and encounters Bobby Lee at the tracks below. The cousins then realize Beth's car has a mystery driver.

Jesse was driving Beth's car and running the liquor himself. As he heads for Florence, a revenuer (Jerry Randall) caught up with him. In an attempt to shake him, Jesse pulls off into the woods. The patch of trees have since been cut down to make room for homes as seen above. When the detour doesn't work, Jesse turns sharply at the bridge below, watching as the revenuer runs off the bridge, crashing into the water.

Tranquil Cemetery is one of the least changed filming sites used in *Moonrunners,* and it truly lives up to its name. Located about a mile off of Georgia Highway 16, the cemetery is tucked into the woods. This is where Jesse's funeral scene was filmed. Many of the funeral attendees were Haralson locals. Bill Estes and his daughter were among the extras. You can see Mr. Estes standing next to Zeebo as the camera pans around. He is wearing a white necktie.

Lee, Grady, and Zeebo break into Jake's cotton gin in order to get even with Jake. The goal was to destroy the liquor Jake was storing and planned to sell to the syndicate. These interior shots were taken in the Haralson Gin, which was operating at the time of filming. This is not the gin that was later blown up.

The last scene of *Moonrunners* is the morning after Bobby Lee, Grady, and Zeebo have blown up Jake's gin. The above shelter is all that is left of the gin that Bob Shelley blew up during filming. The property was slated to be demolished, so the crew (sensing an opportunity to save money) obtained permission from W.C. Adamson to do the work for him. Several locals remembered the explosion; it happened around four in the morning and was so strong that many windows in nearby houses were blown out.

Guide to *Moonrunners* Filming Locations

This section will provide you with directions so that you can tour the filming locations for yourself. Haralson and Williamson are conveniently located an hour south of Atlanta and about twenty minutes west of Griffin, Georgia. There are other points of interest in this area that you may want to visit, so be sure to plan your trip accordingly.

The GPS coordinates for several major filming locations are located below. Use them with caution however; different GPS systems will interpret coordinates differently. The best way to ensure that you see all the filming locations is to use the driving directions that follow on the next page.

Hagg Farmhouse: 33°13'17.85"N 84°35'31.14"W

Jake Rainey's Cotton Gin: 33°13'33.30"N 84°34'12.67"W

Cotton Gin that is blown up: 33°11'6.07"N 84°21'34.75"W

Start of Zeebo and Bobby Lee's Race: 33°13'34.02"N 84°34'10.02"W

Revenuer's Crash into Creek: 33°13'17.88"N 84°36'5.70"W

Cemetery where Jessie is buried: 33°19'30.27"N 84°37'7.58"W

Road blocks: 33°14'53.83"N 84°37'3.72"W

Four way intersection with logging area: 33°14'10.59"N 84°33'42.87"W

Rosco's Courthouse: 33°26'53.16"N 84°27'16.49"W

Driving Directions for Filming Locations

This driving tour will start at either the Marathon or Flash Food gas stations at the intersection of GA-74/GA-85 and GA-16. As soon as you make a right onto GA-16 West, set your trip odometer to 0.0 miles. Begin traveling West on GA-16 toward Newnan. Follow GA-16 for 4.9 miles and turn right onto Standing Rock Road. Continue straight onto Tranquil Road at 5.0 miles. Tranquil Road will become Tranquil Cemetery Road at 5.2 miles; you should bear left here. When your odometer trips 5.4 miles you will be in the cemetery where Jesse Hagg is buried at the end of the film. This is private property; please do not disturb anything on the property or trespass in any way.

Turn around at the entrance of the cemetery and head back up Tranquil Cemetery Road. At 5.6 miles, bear right onto Tranquil Road. At 5.8 miles, you will stay straight as the road becomes Standing Rock Road. Continue straight over GA-16 onto Elder's Mill Road; your odometer should read 5.9 miles. At 9.3 miles, pull over on the right shoulder. Just beyond the fence is Elder's Grist Mill Dam where Bobby Lee and Beth further their relationship. This is private property; do not cross the fence. Pull back onto Elder's Mill Road and continue straight.

At 10.5 miles, bear left onto Gordon Road. There are numerous locations on this road, so you will be stopping frequently. At 11.0 miles, pull over to the side at the intersection of Al Roberts Road. This is where a road block was set up during Zeebo and Bobby Lee's first race. Pull back onto Gordon Road and continue straight. At Nixon Road (11.8 miles), pull on the right shoulder. This is the dirt road where Bobby Lee and Grady escape the police, but get caught by Jake's men. As this is a private road, do not travel down it. The bridge just ahead of you is also featured twice in the film. Pull back onto Gordon Road and cross the bridge. This is where Sheriff Roscoe Coltrane parked his police car with "just enough room" for Zeebo to bust through.

At 12.0 miles, you can pull into the housing division's turn lane to see the hillside where Bobby Lee avoids getting caught. If you look behind you at the bridge you just crossed, you'll see the angle used by filmmakers to capture Zeebo's race with Bobby Lee and Grady. The bridge was used as a road block, which Zeebo burst through to lure the boys into Jake's waiting hands. Continue straight on Gordon Road until it ends.

At 15.2 miles, make a left on GA 74/85. At 15.5 miles, pull into the Dollar General parking lot; the cinder block building at the entrance of the Dollar General lot was used as the Boar's Nest in the film. It is currently used as an auto shop. Please do not disturb the owners of the tire shop or block their driveway. The large ditch that is now in front of the building was not there when the crew filmed in 1973; that was later created for proper drainage when the Dollar General was built. Turn around and make a left back on GA 74/85; your odometer should read 15.6 miles. At 18.7 miles, pull into the entrance of Musick Park Drive. The grassy area to your right is where Jake Rainey's truck stop once stood. Turn around here, make a left on GA 74/85, and continue straight.

Turn left on Rising Star Road at 21.3 miles. Pull on the right shoulder at 21.9 miles. This is the four way intersection where Bobby Lee spins out into the lumber yard trying to lose Jake's men. Continuing on Dead Oak Road, you will come to a sharp right turn at 22.6 miles. This is where the white car slides into the ditch while pursuing Bobby Lee. Use extreme caution when entering this turn.

At 22.7 miles, you will come to a sharp left turn, this was also filmed as part of the Bobby Lee chase scene. Make a left at 22.7 miles, then make an immediate right at 22.8 miles. Bear left around the corner and look to your far left. That metal building was used as Roy Adderholt's barn; Zeebo and Bobby Lee load their cars with shine to deliver to Jake Rainey's truck stop here.

Still at 22.8 miles, bear right onto Railroad Street. All of these small roads were used in the Bobby Lee chase scene. Many of the buildings can be seen in the film. The right you make at 22.9 miles on Line Creek Road is where Bobby Lee slams into the other car causing them both to slide onto the rail road tracks. As you cross the tracks at 22.9 miles, you can see the driveway where Grady pulls out just behind the red and white silos. This is the back entrance to Grady's garage. This is a private business, please do not block traffic into their driveway.

Continue straight on Line Creek Road, and make a left on GA 74/85 at 23.0 miles. At 23.3 miles, turn right on Al Roberts Road. Just at the crest of the hill (23.4 miles) pull over on the right shoulder to see the long stretch of road where Bobby Lee begins his decoy run and Jake's men pull out behind him. Continue straight on Al Roberts Road. At 24.2 miles, you should pull over. On your left is what is left of the Hagg Farmhouse. While you may take pictures, do not explore the property. It is privately owned and all trespassing is forbidden and will be prosecuted.

The intersection just ahead (24.3 miles) is where Bobby Lee stops Beth Ann's car after backing into the biker bar and falls out laughing. The road to your right is Glaizer Road. Many car stunts were filmed on this road, however, with the changing landscape is is difficult to pinpoint where some of the stunts took place. Continue straight on Al Roberts. At 24.7 miles, you will cross the bridge where Jesse makes a sharp left turn during his moonshine run, causing the pursuing revenuer to drive off the bridge into the creek. Continue driving straight to make a safe turn around in the intersection you reach at 25.4 miles. This intersection was also used in filming. A revenuer comes over the crest of the hill to your left in pursuit before swinging onto the dirt road behind you.

After turning around, head back up Al Roberts Road the way you came. At 27.6 miles, make a right on GA 74/85. At 31.1 miles, make a left on 362 at Alvaton. We will now be heading to Williamson, Georgia to see the remaining filming locations. At 37.8 miles, bear right (look for the Hollonville Opry). At 44.0 miles, pull into the shops on the left at Howard Street. There is a small parking lot on your right across the street from the gas station if you'd prefer to park there. This is where Zeebo meets Bobby Lee and Grady and challenges them to a race. Making a left back on 362, you'll make another left on Midland Street at 44.2 miles. At 44.3 miles, you can pull into the dirt drive on your right. This is where the cotton gin that was blown up at the end of the film once stood. Now a private business, please do not explore the property. Turn around here.

Make a left back onto Midland Street and an immediate left on 362 (44.4 miles). Follow 362 to GA 19. You'll take the left for 19 North at 49.5 miles. Griffin is approximately five miles ahead.

Appendix

Moonrunners Credits

Brian W. Roy's *American Cinematographer* Article

Farnum Gray's review of *Moonrunners* from *The Atlanta Constitution*

Acknowledgements

References

"Moonrunners"
1975

Director: Gy Waldron
Written by: Gy Waldron

Musical Director: Waylon Jennings

James Mitchum ... Grady Hagg
Kiel Martin ... Bobby Lee Hagg
Arthur Hunnicutt ... Uncle Jesse Hagg
Chris Forbes ... Beth Ann Eubanks
George Ellis ... Jake Rainey, Bootlegger
Pete Munro ... Zeebo, Bootlegger
Joan Blackman ... Reba Rainey
Waylon Jennings ... The Balladeer
Ralph Mooney ... Steel Guitar and Drums
Don Brooks ... Harmonica
Fred Newell ... Himself - lead guitar, banjo
Larry Whitemore ... Rhythm guitar
Duke Goff ... Bass guitar
Richie Albright ... Percussion
Elaine "Spanky" McFarlane ... Precious
Joey Giardello ... Syndicate Man
Rick Hunter ... Rowdy Boar's Nest patron
Dick Steinborn ... Obnoxious bar patron
Happy Humphrey ... Tiny
John Chappell ... Luther
Bill Moses ... Federal Agent in charge
Bob Hannah ... Roy Adderholt
Bruce Atkins ... Sheriff Roscoe Coltrane
Bobby Dunn ...
Edie Kramer ... Truckstop girl
Anita Allen ...
Lois Zeitlin ... Truckstop girl
Kay Simpson ...

Bill Gribble ... Cooter Pettigrew
James Beard ... Minister
Phil Pleasants ... Cooter's brother
Ben Jones ... Fred
John Clower ... L.D.
Rhona Pope ...
Pattie Shaw ... Boar's Nest patron
Laura Frost ...
Grace McEachron ...
Cathy Rushing ...
Jerry Rushing ... Jake Rainey's bodyguard (uncredited)

Produced By: Robert B. Clark

Cinematography by: Brian Roy
Film Editing by: Avrum Fine
Art Direction by: Pat Mann

Production Management: Peter Cornberg

Second Unit Director: Don Walters

Sound Department: Joe Clayton, Jim Hawkins

Special Effects by: Bob Shelley

Stunts: Mike Head, Charles Mincey, Jerry Rushing, Gene Witham,
Jerry Randall, Jim Hogan

Still Photographer: Betty Bennett
Key Grip: Jim Latham
Gaffer: Bert Bertolami
Camera Operator: Sean Doyle
Camera Operator: Allen Facemire

Assistant Camera: Bruce MacCallum
Assistant Camera: George Mooradian

Costumes: Pattie Shaw

Supervising Editor: William K. Chulack
Assistant Editor: Dennis Dutton

Production Staff: Bill Britton, Frank Harris, Mike Mosley, Thomas
Oliver, Robert Shelley, Tom Skarda

Sound Engineer: Kyle Lehning

Continuity: Alexandria Fedak

Dialogue Coach: Jim Way

Technical Advisor: Jerry Rushing

'Traveler' courtesy of Mike Head.

Sound: Glen Glenn

Special Promotional Material provided by:
  Wing Archery Company
  Justin Boot Company
  Wrangler Blue Bell
  Holiday Inn of Griffin, Georgia

Special Thanks to:
  W.C. Adamson
  William Estes
  Sheriff. J.A. Jones of Fayette County
  Sheriff G.A. Massey of Cowetta County

"Filming 'Moonrunners'"
by Brian W. Roy

This article first appeared in American Cinematographer .

"Moonrunners" is a contemporary comedy based on the exploits of one-time moonshiner, Jerry Rushing, who also acted as advisor on the film. Written and directed by Gy Waldron and produced by Bob Clark, "Moonrunners" was photographed entirely on location about 40 miles southwest of Atlanta, in and around a small town called Haralson. The entire cast and crew stayed in nearby Griffin for six weeks.

When Gy first called me, he suggested that he would like to shoot in black and white, because as he explained, although "Moonrunners" is a comedy, he did not want it to have a "high-key." super-slick look, which he felt would be the effect of shooting in color. He was concerned that it would only detract from the feeling of reality necessary to the story.

He had already chose many of his locations, both interior and exterior, after making many trips to the Haralson area. I went with him later and we drove many miles over narrow country roads that would used in some of the high-speed car chases. We also looked at some old houses, including the one that would be the home of Jesse, played by Arthur Hunnicutt, one of the main characters in the story. Built in 1868, this house was occupied by Mr. And Mrs. Quick, both in the seventies, and just as charming and hospitable as they could be.

This, together with the other locations we looked at, were so rustic and full of character, I didn't feel that black and white would do them justice. I assured Gy that I would try to light in such a manner as to retain as closely as possible the quality and character for which he chose the locations. I also discussed with Movielab in New York, the fact that I wanted to underexpose some of my interiors by two stops and force-develop one stop, my reasons being that I felt I could achieve the look I wanted from a thin negative rather than depending on the lab to give me what I wanted from a normal negative. Surprisingly, they did not scream at the suggestion. In fact, they were extremely cooperative. Our work print was excellent and Gy was very pleased with how the interiors looked.

We hear a great deal about archiving an authentic or natural look on film, I believe that, like beauty, it is in the eye of the beholder. I think we achieved our goal in this respect and hope that the audience will think so, too. We spent about six days shooting in and around the Quick house, and the first members of the crew to arrive early each morning were welcomed by the Quicks with hot coffee and biscuits. The house was supported by large boulders all around which appeared to have been placed strategically wherever the house looked as though it was about to collapse. Inside, the floors undulated throughout. You could even see all the way through to the ground between some of the boards... The house is still standing and probably will for another one hundred years.

We shot both in the kitchen and in the living room. In the kitchen, we shot several "day scenes" and several "night scenes." Our blocking for the day scenes was such that at some point, we would be seeing the windows. I decided to use 85ND3 so they would not burn out. This left the outside hotter, but you could still see the detail. Inside I used two 1K soft lights, one above each window. This gave me a working aperture of T/4 at ASA 200. In approaching the lighting from this standpoint, we were trying to retain the appearance of the kitchen as it originally looked. I believed we achieved this.

As for the night scenes, our apparent source was from a bare bulb hanging in the middle of the kitchen, which never actually appeared in the shot. I don't like to show a bare bulb unless it is absolutely necessary. Sometimes it is, but in this case, I felt that the apparent source was believable without showing it. It is important to the realism of the scene that the key light be determined by the position of the apparent source... whether it is in front, behind, or to the side of the subject. As an example, we have a scene which takes place at night in Jesse's living room. Kiel Martin, who plays Lee, and Chris Forbes, who plays Beth, are seated on the couch, their backs to the camera. Jesse paces back and forth as he talks to them, thus facing the camera. The practical, a table lamp, is in the corner of the room facing the camera as well. The key light is hung directly above the table lamp so that when Jesse is pacing, he is side-lit at one point;

then, as he moves between the table lamp and the camera, he is completely back-lit, except for a minimal amount of fill light.

I used the same lighting setup for the reverse shots, except for a set light on the wall facing the camera.

One of the biggest and most challenging lighting setups is an abandoned tavern, renamed the "Boar's Nest." It was decorated inside and out by art director Pat Mann and his crew so realistically that many passing motorists stopped in for a cold beer. In other sections of this same building, Mann built a barroom and brothel, which again were fantastic and real-looking. At least, I was told the brothel looked real. The major problem in lighting the tavern was that it was necessary to see the whole room at some point, and the ceiling, would be in the shot, eliminating the possibility of stringing lights. The room was also going to be filled with people sitting at tables and in booths, and some walking around. It was not practical to hid lights behind anyone since they would be constantly moving. I decided to put small practical lamps on all the tables with No. 1 Photofloods inside and cut red gel to fit inside the shades. Those sides of each lamp that faced the camera were scrimmed down so as not to appear too hot. Other areas in this same room such as the bar area and the bandstand, I was able to light from the veiling by placing units behind hanging signs or beams. Bert Bertolami, key grip, and Jim Latham, gaffer, whose speed and experience made this and many other setups seem like a breeze, have a grip and lighting truck that has just about every piece of equipment you could need, and if it isn't there, they'll build it. We used many local people as extras and they were extremely enthusiastic and patient, despite the heat, the smoke, and the logistics involved in shooting such a major scene. Here again, I believe we achieved the desire look. The brothel scene was a similar situation. However, it was decorated rather garishly and had white muslin draped over the entire ceiling, rather like the inside of a tent. Behind the muslin, we placed at various points throughout the ceiling, RFLs, which appeared in the shot and gave a low-key over-all ambient light. Key sources were then placed where they would be most effective. The scene calls for Lee, at the opposite end of the room, to run the entire length of the room and dive into the middle of a bevy of beauties, before Jake, played by George Ellis, comes in and puts an end to the shenanigans.

We have a very funny scene that takes place in the dining room of Jake's house where he and Zeebo, played by Chuck Monroe, are seated facing each other and discussing how Jake has bought the local judge and the Sheriff and how this is going to ensure Zeebo will get through with his load of liquor and Lee and Grady (Jim Mitchum) will be caught. Zeebo's attention is marred by Reba (Joan Blackman), Jake's wife, who keeps flirting with him. This is a very funny scene and I felt that it was necessary to keep it fairly high-key so that none of the facial expressions of the players could be missed. For this scene, I decided to put tracing paper over the windows and out lights outside, three 1000 W quartz units, stacked at each of the two windows which would appear in the shot. Inside I used two 1000 W quartz units, one on Jake, and one on Zeebo, from the window side so as to give a little more contrast and not have them looking too flat. Reba was seated close to one of the windows... The windows did not glare and the overall scene was very pleasing.

In another situation, we had what I believe was a fairly tricky lighting setup. We were shooting in the bikers' hangout, a sort of beer joint, which, in fact, as very small, and had been made out of an old frame house by the art department. When I say small, I mean *small*. I am only 5'4" and I could touch the ceiling. It was full of milling bikers and their "birds" and except for some fill light packed up against the camera, I could put no other units inside. Thus, I had to light through the windows. That still didn't help much. It was like the Black Hole of Calcutta because people were right up against the windows and blocking light from reaching inside the room. Of course, as they moved around, light did spill into the room occasionally. There wasn't much else I could do at this point, even if I'd had the luxury of time, so I decided to have the film flashed. I spoke to my contact at Movielab and explained the situation in detail to him. The film was flashed 10%. I could hardly believe the results. They were way beyond my expectations. I was just about able to see every detail and every face in there without losing anything of the "dingy" quality that Mann and his crew had worked so hard to achieve. On looking at the film, I might have gotten by without flashing, but I didn't feel I could risk it at the time.

Lee and Beth enter the hangout and are confronted by the bikers. Lee ends up having a beer poured over his head, but retains his cool and leaves peacefully with Beth. However, they both return immediately in their car, in reverse at high speed, plunging straight through the wall of the hangout as bikers scatter everywhere. This was covered by three cameras, two inside and one outside.

Among the night scenes called for in the script, were the stock-car racing at the track near Atlanta, and also several car chases on narrow country roads in and around Haralson. The race track was lit by banks of metal-balide lamps around the track. The pit area in the center where there would be a considerable amount of dialogue, had no light whatever. We had only 16 foot candles at the hottest points around the track so I shot tests to determine if it would be possible to shoot with the existing lights, and obtain satisfactory results. I had the lap process one roll normally, the second roll forced one stop, and the their roll forced two stops. The second roll which was forced one stop really looked excellent. The first roll was a little dark and the grain and slight fogging in the third became quite objectionable. So I decided to shoot the dialogue sequences in the pit area as well with 16 foot-candles. This, of course, was necessary in order that though areas around the pit would read. At one particularly dark area on the track, we put up two six-FAYS, but had to kill them when some of the race drivers c complained of being blinded on the corner.

The only "day for night" photography was used on some car chases. Day for night photography, as I think most cameramen will agree, is not very satisfactory. For want of a better description, it almost always looks better exactly like what it is. Again, I shot some tests based on the usual recommendations of removing the 8 filter, underexposing two stops, then processing normal. I shot with the sun in various positions, to the side, three-quarters back, and back, also in complete overcast. The latter was by far the best. During the actual shooting of the chases, we ere fortunate to have overcast skies. We replaced the standard head lights of the cars with high powered beams which helped considerably.

I'd like to mention at this point that all the stunts carried out in the cars were authentic and were based on actually experiences of Jerry Rushing, who did some of the driving in the film. Jerry Randall, a stunt driver from California, performed some of the major stunts in the film and, to say the least, was absolutely amazing. I am sorry to report that Jerry Randall was killed recently in a kite accident.

Director Waldron was careful in making sure all the stunts were believable and that no car would be allowed to continue on when it was obviously "wiped out," as in the case in so many films. We had ten cars, none of which was more than two years old, and all of which had seen some rough service as New Jersey taxi cabs. Frank Harris, our chief mechanic, certainly had his hands full with this lot. Keeping them in shape was a full time job. Some of the star cars, of course, had doubles and as we gradually wiped them out, one by one, it became necessary to use a car for several different purposes. One day a car might belong to a moonshiner and the next day it would be a police car. Harris and his crew spray-painted the cars overnight, and sometimes, they came onto the set still wet. I can only imagine the nightmare that this must have been for production manager Peter Cornberg, who managed to keep track of it all without losing his sanity. He did a fantastic job of keeping it together.

All in all, this was a very smooth shoot by a very professional and enthusiastic crew, who thoroughly enjoyed themselves. We completed filming on schedule and, despite abominable weather, the very last day, we managed to put the final minutes in the can between thunder showers. Just as well, as it rained everyday the following week.

"Director Fails in 'Moonrunners'"
By Farnum Gray
Constitution Entertainment Writer

This article first appeared in The Atlanta Constitution.

"Moonrunners" made in Georgia with a number of Atlanta actors, has a colorful, lively story about an impoverished moonshine clan and their struggle against a crime syndicate, the Internal Revenue Service, and a local crime baron.

Unfortunately, it suffers from a poorly written screenplay and poor direction of actors.

Were the screenplay by someone like William Price Fox, a masterful writer of folksy Southern humor, this could have been a very good move.

Gy Waldron directed the movie and wrote the screenplay.

Arthur Hunnicut, who has played character roles in many westerns, plays Jesse, a man with equally religious devotion to the Bible and the manufacture of untaxed whiskey. He refuses to compromise the quality of his whiskey to increase profits.

Two young men, played by Kiel Martin and Jim Mitchum, aren't much good for anything but messing around with women and cars.

The rural vice baron, Jake, has joined a Mafia-type syndicate. Jesse won't join because the syndicate would dilute the purity of his whiskey. So Jake sets out to crush him.

The normally aimless young men commit themselves to defending Jesse's interests.

Jake is played by George Ellis, proprietor of the Film Forum in Atlanta.

Chris Forbes and Joan Blackman have the top female roles.

Mitchum is the son of Robert Mitchum, the star of an earlier moonshiner movie, "Thunder Road." Despite a strong physical resemblance, the younger Mitchum is a much lesser actor.

Poor acting is so much a part of "Moonrunners" that Waldron's directing has to be at fault.

A clear indicator is the performance of Hunnicut, which ranges from perfunctory to worse. Yet, under Paul Mazusky's direction in "Harry and Tonto," Hunnicut created a striking characterization.

At times, the actors grope awkwardly for their cues. That's common in live productions, but a director has no excuse for letting it happen in a film.

Bruce Atkins, an Atlanta actor, plays the law officer Jake buys. Other Atlantans can be seen in minor parts.

The movie is presented like a country legend, with Waylon Jennings narrating and singing the soundtrack songs. It's a nice touch and Jennings does his part very well.

Despite its faults, the movie has warmth and an ability to provoke nostalgia. I liked Brian Roy's photography of the Southern countryside.

Kiel Martin and Chris Forbes do one of those idyllic scenes of young lovers romping though the countryside, and Roy captures it sensuously and tastefully. As they walk across an old wooden railroad trestle, one can smell the honeysuckle thick around them.

The scenes of car chases and trick driving are fun to watch. They're done better than similar scenes in many movies costing far more.

Acknowledgements

Writing *A Moonrunner's Tale* has been challenging. For a film that was shot in a such a small area, gathering information was unusually difficult. I owe a debt of gratitude to many people for their willingness to share their stories, memories, and snapshots. Though I know I will be forgetting someone, I'd like to thank the following people:

To Jerry Rushing: Thanks for not hanging up on me when I called you far too late in the evening. You are a man among men, and I am so grateful that you were willing to share your life with me.

To Dean Rushing: "Behind every good man is a great woman" must have been written about you.

To Allen Facemire: You have been the "glue" for this project; you led me to Brian, you gave me countless names, and you were always there to answer my inane and numerous questions. For your stories, your lightning sharp memory, your willingness to dig through thousands of negatives, and your incredible generosity, I thank you.

To Brian Roy: Meeting you has been the greatest pleasure. I can honestly say that this book would have never pulled together had it not been for you.

To Bob Shelley: In 2006, you gave me the tip off that started this whole quest. Thank you, thank you, thank you.

To David Allen: Your work on the cover and promotional materials was so greatly appreciated. It's awesome to have such talented friends!

To Cecil Cornett and his crew at American Auto Welding in Smithfield, Virginia: I couldn't be more pleased with your work on my 1971 Plymouth Fury II. Thanks for bringing Bobby Lee's car back to life for me!

I would also like to recognize the following individuals for their contributions to this book:

George Boyd
Joe Clayton
John Clower
Charlie Edwards
Ronald Glazier
Jim Hawkins
Mike Head
Ben Jones
Bruce MacCallum
Spanky McFarlane
Charlie Mincey
George Mooradian
Patricia Poland
Tom Skarda
Eleanor Wilkinson
Frank Wilkinson

References

1. Bowman, James Cloyd. *Pecos Bill: The Greatest Cowboy of All Time*. New York: New York Review of Books, 2007.
2. Wolfe, Tom. "The Last American Hero Is Junior Johnson." *Esquire*. March 1965: 68-74.
3. Forbes, R. J.. *A Short History of the Art of Distillation from the Beginnings up to the Death of Cellier Blumenthal*. 1970.
4. Gately, Iain. *Drink: A Cultural History of Alcohol*. New York: Penguin Group, 2008.
5. Grose, Francis. *A classical of the vulgar tongue*. 1785.
6. Hogeland, Willam. *The Whiskey Rebellion*. New York: Simon and Schuster, 2006.
7. Hogeland, 2006.
8. Hogeland, 2006.
9. Hogeland, 2006.
10. Gusfield, Joseph R.. *Symbolic Crusade: Status Politics and the American Temperance Movement*. Chicago: University of Illinois Press, 1986.
11. Zimmerman, Jonathan. "The Queen of the Lobby": Mary Hunt, scientific temperance, and the dilemma of democratic education in America, 1879-1906. *History of Education Quarterly*, 1992, *32*, p. 6.
12. Pietrusza, David. *1920: The Year of Six Presidents*. New York: Carroll and Graf, 2007.
13. Friedrich, Otto. Hays Gorey. Ruth Mehrtens Galvin. "F.D.R.'S Disputed Legacy." *Time*. February 1, 1982. Retrieved January 15, 2010.
14. Orkent, Daniel. *Great Fortune: The Epic of Rockefeller Center*. New York: Viking Press, 2003. 246/7.
15. Willis, Ken. "Fork in the Road." *Auto Racing Digest*. Mar 2001.
16. Records from The General Court of Justice Superior Court Division. June 17 Session, 1974. State of North Carolina. County of Union.
17. Maltin, Leonard. *Leonard Maltin's 2009 Movie Guide*. New York: Penguin Group, 2008.

18. Hofstede, David. *The Unofficial Companion: The Dukes of Hazzard*. Los Angeles: Renaissance Books, 1998.
19. Hofstede, 1998.
20. McNary, Dave. Tatiana Siegel. "Fox's 'Watchmen' lawsuit heats up." *Variety*. August 18, 2008. Retrieved on January 15, 2010.
21. Brodesser, Claude. "Warners ponies up 'Hazzard' pay." *Variety*. June 29, 2005. Retrieved on January 15, 2010.

CPSIA information can be obtained at www.ICGtesting.com
Printed in the USA
BVOW04s1801011013

332620BV00001B/226/P